Manchester

at War 1939–45

Your Towns and Cities in World War Two

Manchester
at War 1939–45

Glynis Cooper

Pen & Sword
MILITARY

First published in Great Britain in 2018 by
PEN & SWORD MILITARY
An imprint of
Pen & Sword Books Ltd
47 Church Street
Barnsley
South Yorkshire
S70 2AS

ISBN 978-1-47387-575-3

A CIP catalogue record for this book is available from the British Library.

Typeset by Concept, Huddersfield, West Yorkshire HD4 5JL.
Printed and bound in England by CPI Group (UK) Ltd, Croydon CR0 4YY.

Pen & Sword Books Ltd incorporates the imprints of Pen & Sword Archaeology, Atlas, Aviation, Battleground, Discovery, Family History, History, Maritime, Military, Naval, Politics, Railways, Select, Social History, Transport, True Crime, and Claymore Press, Frontline Books, Leo Cooper, Praetorian Press, Remember When, Seaforth Publishing and Wharncliffe.

For a complete list of Pen & Sword titles please contact
PEN & SWORD BOOKS LIMITED
47 Church Street, Barnsley, South Yorkshire, S70 2AS, England
E-mail: enquiries@pen-and-sword.co.uk
Website: www.pen-and-sword.co.uk

Contents

Dedication

To my father, Edmund Cooper, and my mother, Joyce Plant, two Mancunians whose lives and destinies were shaped by the Second World War, and who were ultimately its victims as much as those killed in action; to all those Mancunians who suffered, fought and died in the war as well as those who gave so much on the Home Front; and to the City of Manchester, much of it reduced to smoking ruins by the German Blitz, which rose like a phoenix from its ashes to become the splendid, vibrant city it is today.

Acknowledgments

Many thanks to Manchester Central Library, the Imperial War Museum North, those who had living memory of the war and talked about what it was really like; my long-suffering family and friends, and the equally long-suffering editorial team at Pen & Sword; Roni Wilkinson who commissioned the book; and to my daughters and their curiosity about a war they never knew but which robbed them prematurely of their grandparents.

Introduction

Manchester at War 1939–45 deals with the City (centre) of Manchester and its thirty 'inner' immediately surrounding suburbs. These include: Ancoats, Ardwick, Beswick, Blackley, Bradford, Burnage, Cheetham, Chorlton-cum-Hardy, Chorlton-on-Medlock, Clayton, Collyhurst, Crumpsall, Didsbury, Fallowfield, Gorton, Harpurhey, Hulme, Levenshulme, Longsight, Miles Platting, Moss Side, Moston, Newton Heath, Northenden, Openshaw, Rusholme, Victoria Park, Whalley Range, Withington and Wythenshawe. The 'outer' suburbs of nine towns and the present Metropolitan Borough Councils (MBCs) include: Trafford, Salford, Wigan, Bolton, Bury, Rochdale, Oldham, Tameside and Stockport, which currently (2018) constitute Greater Manchester, but were then separate entities and consequently are not included in this book. Manchester's twin city, Salford, is not included either, although Salford had similar experiences, especially in the Blitz, and was bombarded with Nazi propaganda leaflets dropped from aircraft at the outbreak of the war. The boundary between the two cities is the River Irwell but Salford was, and still is, a very separate entity and has its own stories to tell. The Great War had cost Manchester dearly and it was hoped the years following its end would see Manchester's trade and industries recover, and consequently improve conditions for its citizens. Although its engineering industries made some recovery, Manchester was dealt a huge blow by the relentless decline of its cotton industry. America, India and Japan had been slowly buying up British cotton-manufacturing machinery and railway rolling stock since the 1880s and they had started their own cotton-manufacturing industries. This resulted in undercutting on prices, loss of trade, and when Japan started 24-hour working of their cotton mills in the early 1920s it meant that they could fulfil orders far more quickly and cheaply than the UK. In 1930 the Cotton Board established the practice of choosing annual 'cotton queens', young, attractive, vibrant, cotton workers to travel and promote the industry and its products. But it was too little, too late.

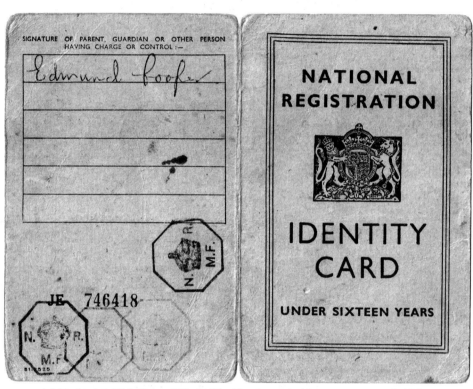

A Manchester child's Second World War identity card. All men, women and children were required to carry identity cards at all times during the War.

CHAPTER ONE

Background to the Renewed Outbreak of World War

This time the threat of war did not creep up on the nation almost unnoticed. The signs had been there since the end of the 'war to end all wars'. Those returning from the Great War did not find the promised 'land fit for heroes' but one of high unemployment, an acute housing shortage, food rationing and massive national debt. It provoked the inevitable backlash; first against women for taking men's jobs and, secondly, racial attacks on Jews and Belgian refugees for also stealing jobs; followed by anger at the practically bankrupt state of the country. Women, who had been the sole breadwinners, were thrown out of their jobs and replaced by men, leaving many with no means of supporting themselves. Any female resistance was often met by derision, sometimes a good beating, and, occasionally, rape. Women now had a stronger political voice since being given the vote in 1918, although this was still selective, but universal suffrage, that is the right to vote for all citizens in Britain aged 21 and over (the minimum voting age is now 18) except criminals and the insane, was granted in 1928. Mine and mill owners, desperate to retain their wealth, reduced workers' wages to try and maintain the status quo. Many had lost money by investing in war loans and bonds during the Great War, attracted by the high returns, promises that of course the government could not meet. In 1925 the UK restored the Gold Standard which adversely affected exports due to extra levies and taxes. In turn this badly affected the mining industry whose workers had seen their wages reduced to almost half of their original level by mine owners desperate to retain profits. The General Strike of May

1926 was led by the miners but it received wide support from many other industries. Conditions did not improve, however, and then came the Wall Street Crash in the autumn of 1929. This had a knock-on effect on British banks and the UK withdrew from the Gold Standard in 1931. These events precipitated the Great Depression of the 1930s. Unemployment doubled and there was much poverty and widespread food shortages. The Jarrow Hunger March of 1936 took place when 200 men from the Tyneside town of Jarrow marched to London asking for re-establishment of industry in the town after the closure of its shipyard. They were led by Ellen Wilkinson, a Mancunian who at that time was MP for Jarrow, but who became Minister of Education just after the end of the war. In December of that year the new king, Edward VIII, abdicated to marry the woman he loved, an American lady already twice divorced. His younger brother, Bertie, the father of Queen Elizabeth II, ascended the throne as King George VI.

At the same time, a politician named Adolf Hitler, who had fought during the Great War, was rapidly rising to power in Germany. The 1919 Treaty of Versailles had humiliated and economically crippled Germany. In their eagerness and desire for revenge and reparations, the Allies had insisted that the Treaty should be drawn up and signed as quickly as possible so that Germany would not cause more trouble. As a result of this haste, the Weimar Republic and its attendant constitution had loopholes enabling someone like Hitler to take advantage. By 1937 his Nuremburg Rallies were beginning to cause disquiet in Britain. The rallies were an annual event to attract and inspire members of his Nazi Party. There was alarm about the wild fervour displayed by Hitler when addressing these rallies and it caused great concern to a large number of people. In June that year, the abdicated king, Edward (now known as the Duke of Windsor), married his sweetheart, Wallis Simpson, in France, and they began their honeymoon in a railway coach lent by the Italian dictator Benito Mussolini. This writer's grandparents, both Mancunians, refused to allow her aunt (a nursery teacher who lived and worked in neighbouring Stockport) to go on holiday to Germany in 1937 because they simply did not trust Hitler and his henchmen. In the autumn that same year the Duke and Duchess of Windsor visited Hitler at Berchtesgaden, his private home in the Alps; and they returned to Germany for another visit the following year. Germany was bitter about the territory she had been obliged to forfeit as part of the Treaty of Versailles and now Hitler's foreign policy was becoming more aggressive. In 1938 he annexed Austria and threatened to invade the Sudetenland (the border districts of Czechoslovakia). The British Prime Minister, Neville Chamberlain, took an approach of appeasement, agreeing to the Sudetenland annexation if that was the limit of Hitler's territorial ambitions. Hitler, playing Chamberlain perfectly, agreed and the 'Munich Agreement' was signed. Chamberlain returned to England to make his famous 'peace in our time' speech at the House of Commons. There was now serious unease about the Duke of Windsor's seemingly close connections with the Third Reich. The Duke claimed, however, that he and the Duchess had simply been misled about Hitler and the Nazi Party's real intentions. Many Mancunians shook their heads in disbelief. If even they could see the way the wind was blowing, then surely their former king could have done so. However, it has to be remembered that the Duke's family was of exclusively German descent on both sides and had been since 1714 (with the sole exception of his grandmother, Queen Alexandra, who was a Danish princess); a fact of which his father, King George V, had been painfully aware in the Great War when he changed the family's German surname of Saxe-Coburg-Gotha to the rather more English-sounding one of Windsor. It might have simply been a case of family history and background blinding the Duke of Windsor to the ugly realities and ambitions of the Third Reich. Despite the Munich Agreement, in March 1939, Hitler invaded the rest of Czechoslovakia. There was now great concern that Poland would be next on his list. It was a step too far for the French and the British, and an ultimatum was issued by both countries that he should not invade Poland. This was ignored by Hitler, who invaded Poland on 1 September. He was given a deadline by the British of 11.00am on 3 September by which time assurances were to have been received that all German troops had been withdrawn from Poland or Britain would declare war on Germany once more. Nothing was heard and at 11.15am Neville Chamberlain broadcast to the nation on radio. Quietly, he explained the situation and then continued 'I have to tell you now that no such undertaking has been received and consequently this country is at war with Germany'.

CHAPTER TWO

1939

Manchester had been given its own insight into fascism during the early 1930s. Oswald Mosley, a former member of the Labour Party who had become disillusioned with its policies, had formed his own party, the New Party, and had stood as its candidate in the Ashton-under-Lyne by-election in 1931. Ashton is now subsumed into Greater Manchester but in 1931 it was still a separate Lancashire town some 7 or 8 miles from the city. Mosley did not win the seat and the New Party took a disturbingly extreme direction, becoming radical and authoritarian and sympathetic to fascist policies. 'Para-military security guards' wearing black shirts patrolled its meetings which further increased the general sense of unease.

However, for Manchester, the fight against fascism had begun well before the declaration of war in September 1939, and reactions in the city to Mosley and his henchmen were influenced by the experiences of those who had joined the International Brigades to fight on the side of the Republicans against Franco during the Spanish Civil War (1936–9). A number of young men volunteered from the Manchester area, over fifty coming from the city and its immediate suburbs; but what really captured the Manchester public's attention were the activities of the city's women who had volunteered to work as nurses in the Civil War, and of a particular one from Chorlton-cum-Hardy named Madge Addy. In 1937 she was working as a nurse at a hospital in Castile, and like other nurses took part in fundraising campaigns. Ellen Wilkinson, a Mancunian born in Chorlton-on-Medlock and educated in Ardwick, later a Labour MP who led the Jarrow Hunger March, set up the Spanish Medical Aid Committee of which there was a branch in North Manchester. Madge Addy donated blood to save Spanish soldiers and helped in developing techniques for collecting and storing blood by the Republican medical services which also helped save lives during the Second World War. She made desperate appeals to her home city for food, clothes and medical supplies for her patients, saying '... please ask Manchester to do its utmost to send money so that necessary stuff can be bought ... but don't send anything for me, devote every penny to the hospital ...'. There were also a number of Spanish and Portuguese Jews in Manchester so that there was an additional vested interest in the Spanish Civil War, but many Manchester folk were politically aware, in addition to the fact that Manchester men were fighting against Franco. Manchester women like Winifred Horrocks and Bessie Berry campaigned vigorously for aid for Spain. Winifred Horrocks led the Manchester 'Foodship for Spain' project and organized an exhibition of Picasso's painting 'Guernica', the entrance fees from which were used to fund the 'Foodship' campaign. Bessie Berry campaigned for Aid Spain and married Sam Wild, commander of the British Battalion of the International Brigades. Young Mancunians fighting in the Spanish Civil War were shocked by fascist fighting methods and by the ferocity of the bombing attack on Guernica, immortalized in Picasso's painting. It was rumoured that the bombing and carnage at Guernica was a dress-rehearsal for the World War which was to come. Although supposedly neutral during the Second World War, it was no secret that Franco was sympathetic towards Germany and Italy and allowed Spanish resources and access routes to be used by the Axis Powers. Near Alhaurin el Grande, in Andalusia, a house in a remote valley was rumoured to have been used for secret wartime meetings between Franco, Hitler and Mussolini. The entrance to the valley was hidden and difficult to access but the remains of sentry posts, fortifications and residential buildings were still clearly visible in 2009. Today, however, the trees have been cut down and the valley re-developed so that a fascinating story will always remain just that, a story worthy of 'Boy's Own' or James Bond. Ernest Hemingway wrote *For Whom the Bell Tolls*, the tale of a young American who joins an anti-fascist guerrilla unit in the Spanish Civil War, which was published in 1940 to great acclaim, and echoed the experiences of the British freedom fighters in Spain. General Franco, like Hitler, took the view that people were either for him or against him. Those that were against him suffered harshly. Remote caves in Spain are full of the bones of massacred Republican fighters. Many are still listed simply as missing in action but, in the interests of maintaining civil order, the Spanish government is reluctant to launch any public inquiries or organize searches. Approximately a million Spaniards, who had fought against

St Peter's Square, Manchester, on the eve of the Second World War.

Franco, were sent to German concentration camps during the war by Hitler as a favour to Franco. The fate of many remains unknown. A number were sent to the camp on Alderney in the Channel Islands. One of those who survived married a girl from Jersey and wrote a memoir of his experiences.

Oswald Mosley, his Blackshirts and his New Party of fascist believers were not generally well received in Manchester. Mancunians who had opposed fascism in Spain were bitterly and openly critical of Franco's fascists working in co-operation with the German and Italian fascists. This resulted in the New Party, which was greatly sympathetic to the fascist cause, losing both sympathy and supporters. The methods used by the Blackshirts to silence those who did not agree with them had echoes of the oppression the freedom-fighters had witnessed in Spain. Men were battered and beaten up. Women were manhandled and mistreated. However, Mosley came to speak at the Free Trade Hall in Manchester and it was clear that not only was he a powerful orator but he had the kind of charisma and fervour which captured people. The *Manchester Guardian* described his effect on Manchester folk at the meeting:

> When Sir Oswald Mosley sat down ... the audience, stirred as an audience rarely is, rose and swept a storm of applause towards

the platform. Who could doubt that here was one of those root-and-branch men who have been thrown up from time to time in the religious, political and business story of England. First that gripping audience is arrested, then stirred, and finally ... swept off its feet by a tornado or peroration yelled at the defiant high pitch of a tremendous voice.

It was a salutary lesson for Mancunians, many of whom disliked Mosley intensely. Almost equally disliked was William Joyce. He was born in America to an Irish father and a Lancashire mother but had been brought up in County Galway in the Irish Republic. He joined the British Union of Fascists (BUF) in 1932 and he had a powerful skill in oratory. 'Thin, pale, intense, he had not been speaking many minutes before we were electrified by this man ... so terrifying in its dynamic force, so vituperative, so vitriolic ...', wrote the novelist Cecil Roberts. Joyce also developed a violent dislike and distrust of Jewish people. His second wife, Margaret, was a typist from Carlisle who had a Mancunian accent. Sharing her husband's views, she went with him when he left England for Germany to pledge his allegiance to the enemy during the war. Joyce became known as 'Lord Haw Haw' for his radio broadcasts to England from Germany and Margaret became known as 'Lady Haw Haw' when she joined in them. Quite why they both hated England so much wasn't really clear.

Mosley had founded the British Union of Fascists whose chief supporters included Henry Williamson, author of *Tarka the Otter*, and William Joyce, who took a positive delight in taunting the British throughout the war over German successes and Allied defeats. Mosley attracted attention from a number of right wing groups and by 1934 the BUF was a strong and active organization which had gained the support of Lord Rothermere and the *Daily Mail*. Rothermere wrote an article called 'Hurrah for the Blackshirts' in which he commended Mosley for his 'sound, common sense, Conservative doctrine'. He added:

Timid alarmists all this week have been whimpering that the rapid growth in numbers of the British Blackshirts is preparing the way for a system of rulership by means of steel whips and concentration camps. Very few of these panic-mongers have any personal knowledge of the countries that are already under Blackshirt government. The notion that a permanent reign of terror exists there has been evolved entirely from their own morbid imaginations, fed by sensational propaganda from opponents of the party now in power. As a purely British organization, the Blackshirts will respect those principles of tolerance which are traditional in British politics. They have no prejudice either of class or race. Their recruits are drawn from all social grades and every political party ...

However, to their alarm, Mancunians had begun to realize that the Blackshirts' claim to 'have no prejudice of either class or race' was simply untrue. Under the influence of William Joyce, the BUF had become increasingly anti-Semitic and his verbal attacks upon the Jewish community in Britain had resulted in serious riots in London in 1936. Although there had been some anti-Semitic feeling in Manchester, Mancunians still greatly disliked Mosley and Joyce. There had been Jewish people in England intermittently since the Middle Ages but they had not settled in Manchester until around 1750. The Jewish community tended to congregate in the areas around Shude Hill, Cheetham Hill and Broughton in Manchester. The first synagogue was in Long Millgate, although later there were several synagogues in the city and the Spanish and Portuguese synagogue in Cheetham Hill has become a unique Jewish museum. There had been concern in Manchester during the late eighteenth century that Jewish merchants were buying English cotton-spinning machinery to sell to foreign competitors and there was a great fear of industrial espionage. *Prescott's Manchester Journal* of 1774 contained a warning.

Several Jews ... have for some months past frequented the town under various pretences and some of them have procured spinning machines, looms, dressing machines, cutting knives and other tools used in the manufactures of fustians, cotton velvets, velveteens, and other Manchester goods ... and frequent attempts have been made to entice, persuade, and seduce artificers to go to foreign parts of His Majesty's dominions ... this will be the destruction of the trade in this country unless timely prevented ...

Whatever the truth of this, it was not the Jews, some of whom were indeed tailors and traded in textiles because it was a growing and profitable industry, but the Italians who, in 1820, were initially responsible for reproducing or 'plagiarising' English cotton-spinning machinery in another country. In addition, established English machine manufacturers sold their goods abroad throughout the nineteenth century and into the early twentieth century. They were not overly concerned with the future, more with how much money they could earn through their business interests. One of the biggest business success stories of Jewish origin was nothing to do with any of the traditional Jewish occupations which included moneylending, jewellery, watch-making and pawnbroking. Michael Marks was a Jewish refugee who founded Marks and Spencer with the opening of a penny bazaar in Leeds in 1894. The first Manchester branch of Marks and Spencer opened, appropriately enough in Cheetham Hill, after the Great War. The clothing sold was well made and competitively priced, so Marks and Spencer became a byword for quality. However, this did not deter detractors. A few local right-wing groups in the city were always complaining of so-called Jewish conspiracies and there were a number of anti-Jewish demonstrations. This totally ignored the fact that Jewish Manchester men were serving in the armed forces and Jewish Manchester women were in the Women's Land Army throughout the war. However, some felt that there were echoes of Shylock from Shakespeare's play *The Merchant of Venice* in Jewish commercial interests. The Jewish form of worship also contrasted with that of the Christian Church, although both the Christian and Jewish faiths are Abrahamic religions: i.e. they have a common origin or connection with Abraham and they believe in Jesus, Mary, the prophets and the Ten Commandments. By the time of the Second World War, Manchester had quite a sizeable Jewish population and the city was becoming increasingly concerned, the more so when on the eve of war Mosley announced:

> ... we have said a hundred times that if the life of Britain were threatened we would fight again, but I am not offering to fight in the quarrel of Jewish finance in a war from which Britain could withdraw at any moment she likes, with her Empire intact and her people safe. I am now concerned with only two simple facts. This war is no quarrel of the British people, this war is a quarrel of Jewish finance, so to our people I give myself for the winning of peace ...

Most Mancunians couldn't relate the seizing and occupation of Czechoslovakia and Poland to Jewish finance, but to those who

Bomb damage at the Jewish Hospital in Manchester 1941.
(*Courtesy of Manchester Central Library Local Studies*)

had fought against fascism in the Spanish Civil War, the question of Jewish finance or religion, or indeed anything else Jewish, had nothing whatever to do with the situation. Dictatorship and absolute obedience to the dictator, his whims and his wishes, were the name of the game. They wanted no part of it, and they said so volubly and at length. Mosley then inaugurated the 'Britain First' campaign, holding a rally at Earls Court in July 1939. Shortly afterwards, much to the relief of most Mancunians, the government finally cracked down on the Blackshirts and Mosley was interned in May 1940 and remained in prison for much of the war. Other BUF officials were imprisoned and the party was forcibly disbanded. Subsequently it was discovered that Hitler was well aware that Manchester had a large Jewish population and had drawn up detailed plans for their imprisonment and annihilation after he had conquered Britain as he believed he would. Mancunians were saddened, if not surprised, by the formal declaration of war. They had known in their hearts for some time that it was inevitable.

Memories of the Great War were still strong and the government had decided that it was not going to be tardy in its reactions to the hostilities this time. The 'Home Front' had been resurrected the previous year, in September 1938, during the 'Munich Crisis' when

Manchester city police schoolchildren's gas drill, 1938.
(*Courtesy of Manchester Central Library Local Studies*)

Chamberlain was busy at the Munich conference trying to negotiate with Hitler over the Sudetenland. Civilians had been encouraged to join either the Air Raid Precautions (ARP) or the Auxiliary Fire Service (AFS). The ARP was a response to the common fear, instilled by the events of the Great War, of mass bombing from the air which had terrified millions of people.

In June 1939, the Military Training Act came into force which meant that all young men aged 20 to 21 were now liable to be called up for four years' military service. That same month the Women's Auxiliary Air Service (WAAF) was also established. Those who joined had to be aged between 18 and 43. Initially their main responsibilities involved driving, clerical tasks and cooking but, as the war progressed, these expanded rapidly into other areas. A week before the outbreak of war Parliament had passed the Emergency Powers (Defence) Act 1939, an update of the Defence of Realm Act (DORA) passed in 1914, which essentially gave the government carte blanche to do whatever was necessary to tackle the war situation. The hated blackout regulations were reinstated. All doors and windows were to

Cross Street Manchester on the eve of the Second World War. A 'Real Photograph' postcard taken c.1938.

be covered with heavy dark material, cardboard or paint during the hours of darkness. Street lights were switched off. Traffic lights and vehicle lights were fitted with covers which directed their beams downwards. If the air-raid sirens sounded folk were required to turn off stoves and ovens, shut off water taps and gas valves, disconnect electricity, ensure that the blackout curtains were drawn, and then get themselves to a place of safety. Army reservists were called up and civil defence workers placed on alert. The navy sent its fleet to war stations. Evacuation of children and some adults from the densely populated industrial areas of the city had already begun two days before war was even declared. In total 172,000 children and 23,000 adults were evacuated in the three days from 1–3 September. Unlike the Great War, folk no longer had to gather outside the *Manchester Guardian* offices in Cross Street waiting for news. The first radio broadcasts of news, sport and entertainment had been made in 1920, just after the Great War, and many folk now had radios in their own homes. Mancunians, like everyone else, listened with heavy hearts to the declaration of war with Germany. It was just twenty years since the peace treaty to end the war that would end all wars had been signed. Twenty minutes after the initial announcement of war by Neville Chamberlain, air-raid sirens sounded in London although there was no immediate threat of aerial attack from the Germans. The rest of September was a busy month. Chamberlain formed his War Cabinet and the National Service (Armed Forces) Act was passed requiring that all males aged 18 to 41 were liable for conscription. On 7 September, the National Registration Act was passed introducing identity cards for everyone. By 23 September petrol rationing had begun and on the 27th the Cabinet imposed a rise in income tax and the first war tax. Radio was the main media for many as all television transmissions were suspended. Not many people had television in 1939 but, after the declaration of war, it was decided to switch the Alexandra Palace transmitter to jamming German aircraft navigation frequencies. Alexandra Palace was the BBC television headquarters and was known affectionately as 'Ally Pally'. Television manufacturing facilities were subsequently adapted for making radio and radar equipment. All cinemas were closed in September but soon re-opened as the government realized the need for some sort of entertainment and escape from everyday problems. They also realized that cinemas could be used to promote their own propaganda and a number of short films and documentaries were made for this purpose. Football was badly affected as well and initially professional football was suspended. Although football grounds re-opened in September, those watching games were mostly limited to 8,000 spectators. Britain and France were both purchasing heavily-discounted arms from the America but Britain was turning over many of its manufactories to arms and munitions production. Trafford Park became a centre for manufacturing electronics, aircraft and parts for tanks and guns, while the old Ford factory was utilized to turn out Rolls-Royce aero-engines. Rolls-Royce was a Manchester company which came into being over a dinner in the Midland Hotel attended by Charles Rolls and Frederick Royce in 1904. Folk waited anxiously to see what would happen but the first few months of the war were a strange time for Manchester as they were for many other towns and cities in Britain. The striking characteristic was that simply nothing happened on the military front. Many dubbed it the 'Phoney War' and Winston Churchill himself referred to it as the 'twilight war'. There was no military action on land at all for the first eight months until Germany attacked the Low Countries and France in May 1940. Despite this, lessons had been learned from the Great War and folk were advised to carry a standard-issue gas mask with them at all times.

ARP warden gas-protection clothing, Manchester 1941.
(Courtesy of Manchester Central Library Local Studies)

The government firmly believed that the Germans would use some sort of chemical attack against the civilian population. The gas masks would protect users from gases, bacteria and viruses as they formed a sealed cover over the face, eyes, nose and mouth. The hoods with their filters, tubing and eye shields resembled early diving equipment to the practical eye, or perhaps something not quite of this world to the more imaginative. Adult masks were black but children's masks had brightly-coloured eye pieces and red rubber decorations. Babies

Children in gas masks with an air-raid warden, Manchester 1939.
(Courtesy of Manchester Central Library Local Studies)

had gas helmets and their mothers pumped in air with a bellows. Already by the beginning of 1940 over 38 million gas masks had been issued. It must have been the stuff of nightmares for many children.

Air-raid wardens had special gas masks with a long hose and a speaking box attached to the belt. The government also published

Baby inside gas mask, Manchester, 22 August 1939.
(*Courtesy of Manchester Central Library Local Studies*)

information leaflets on the types of gas they believed the Germans would use in attacks.

However, the 'Phoney War' had lulled folk into a false sense of security and by the beginning of 1940 hardly anyone bothered to carry their mask with them at all times. Seriously worried about this seeming complacency, the government ordered air-raid wardens to carry out monthly gas mask inspections. Those not carrying them would be penalised and those who had lost them would be forced to pay for replacements. It may have been a 'Phoney War' on land but a real war was being fought at sea throughout the period, although this did not really affect Manchester itself. The Second Battle of the Atlantic was one of the most notable campaigns. The first British warship to be lost was the aircraft carrier HMS *Courageous* which was torpedoed and sunk with the loss of 519 lives in September 1939. The following month the battleship HMS *Royal Oak* was sunk in Scapa Flow with the loss of 833 men.

There were reconnaissance and propaganda flights by both the RAF and the Luftwaffe, but no bombing raids or chemical attacks, and folk continued to be lulled into a false sense of security, like the calm before the storm. What hurt more immediately was the first war budget. The standard rate of income tax rose by nearly 30 per cent and there were additional taxes on beer, tobacco and sugar. The Germans had resurrected their Great War policy of attacking British merchant shipping and food prices increased. Consequently bacon, butter and sugar were rationed, followed by meat, fish, tea, jam, biscuits, cereals, cheese, eggs, milk and tinned fruit. As in the Great War, everyone had to register with their local grocers and were then issued with ration cards which had to be produced for each item purchased. It was as though the administrative processes of rationing in the Great War had simply been a trial run, although more food-stuffs were rationed in the Second World War and generally lesser quantities were allowed than in the Great War.

Finally, in May 1940, the Germans invaded France and the Low Countries and subsequently occupied the Channel Islands. This was followed by the Italians joining the war in June 1940 which resulted in Italians on the British mainland being interned as aliens in addition to Germans and Austrians. Manchester had quite a large Italian population living close to the city centre in an area of Ancoats known as Little Italy. Now, finally, the 'Phoney War' was over and the real effects would hit home in Manchester at its very heart.

CHAPTER THREE

1940

The year 1940 brought the very harsh and bloody reality of the Second World War to Manchester in no uncertain terms; inflicting death, distress and a destruction still not forgotten. In May the Local Defence Volunteers (LDV), later renamed the Home Guard and immortalized in the classic television series *Dad's Army*, was formed to defend the Home Front.

Members were local volunteers who were ineligible to serve in the armed forces because they were too old (hence the nickname 'Dad's Army'), too young in some cases or in reserved occupations. They were to be a 'secondary defence force' in case of invasion which would, it was hoped, resist enemy forces for long enough to give the regular army a chance to mount a successful counter-attack. Tom Wintringham, who had been one of the commanders of the British

The Home Guard in Withington, Manchester 1940.
(*Courtesy of Manchester Central Library Local Studies*)

Battalion of the International Brigades in the Spanish Civil War, had written a book suggesting that the Home Guard should be organized along the lines of the International Brigades. After the invasion of France and the Low Countries in May there was a very real fear that the Germans would invade Britain. Coastal areas were the most vulnerable, along with lines of communication and industrial complexes. It was also advocated that local rifle clubs should be formed and that the whole adult population should be trained in the use of arms and given weapons. This caused great alarm in government and military circles because it might unleash forces that would be beyond their control. Consequently, the Home Office insisted it was the duty of the army to deal with enemy invaders and that any civilians who shot German troops faced immediate execution themselves. On 14 May, the Secretary of State for War, Anthony Eden, made a radio announcement calling on men aged between 17 and 65 who were not in the armed forces, but still wished to help defend their country, to enrol in the LDV which became known as the Home Guard from late July. Some 250,000 men volunteered in the first week. Eden had wanted 500,000 to volunteer for the Home Guard but while the government were debating details, the ordinary people of the country took matters into their own hands and 1.5 million men had volunteered their services by July. In Manchester there were 7,000 applications in the first few days after Eden's broadcast, and, by the end of the month, there were eleven battalions to cover the area of what is now known as Greater Manchester. The main areas covered by the scope of this book are E Battalion (commanding officer Captain Nichols) served the city centre, F Battalion (Captain Rothband) served Withington, and G Battalion (Captain Simpson) served Wythenshawe. Members of the Home Guard were eventually issued with uniforms, rifles and ammunition, and attended regular drills. In Manchester, they patrolled streets, railway lines and key locations such as airfields, factories and explosives stores, as well as keeping watch for enemy invaders and helping out during bombing attacks or similar emergencies. During the Blitz on Manchester at Christmas 1940 the Home Guard performed invaluable services in firefighting, rescue work, guarding streets and buildings, traffic control, and any other way in which they could help.

The government reminded folk of the importance of civil defence, and of the need to remember the demands on shipping and to be as economical as possible. It was recommended that luxury goods should be restricted, woollen clothing should be reserved for military rather than civilian use, and consumption of bacon and sugar should be reduced. The space taken up on ships by these items could then be used for cargoes of steel or machine tools. Thanks to the 'Phoney War' and the lack of action on land the government felt many folk had failed to realize the severity of the threat that was facing the country. People were more concerned with the day-to-day business of living, of paying increased taxation, and of coping with the rising cost of living. The problem of the black market and profiteers had already been recognized at government level and the Prices of Goods Act had been passed to curtail, if not completely abolish, the mean and miserable practice of making a fortune by withholding supplies until prices were forced up. There were also local industrial issues. Lancashire cotton goods still had an excellent reputation for quality worldwide, but the cotton trade in Manchester was suffering and cotton manufacturers were keen to emphasize the importance of the export trade in wartime. There were problems, however, involving pressures of demand, shortage of supplies, rising prices, dislocation of workers, delivery difficulties and trade outlets, and, as the year progressed, cotton exports continued to fall. It may be clearer with hindsight but the death knell had already sounded for the cotton trade after the Great War, mainly due to American, Indian and Japanese competition, failure to source alternative supplies of raw materials and the loss of the Eastern markets after they had set up their own cotton-manufacturing industries. The Cotton Board was keen to institute a five-year plan for future development and success but this would rely on government support and the question of wages. There was already discontent among workers about the level of wages in regard to the rising costs of living but the Lancashire cotton trade could not compete on wage levels with other areas of the world where very low wages were paid. The Cotton Board was anxious to resolve that discrepancy by the volume of export trade and differential pricing rather than controlled pricing. It was an optimistic outlook which hindsight shows was sadly not successful. However, the iron and steel industries in Manchester were faring rather better. Although there was a shortage of cast iron scrap, there were larger quantities of pig iron available and the general engineering foundries were doing well, as were their more specialized counterparts. The finished iron trade was also doing well. Conditions in the steel industry had remained largely unchanged, and the demand for tanks, boilers, rollers, structural steel materials and special alloy steels remained constant, ensuring capacity working.

On 10 June Fascist Italy joined the war on the side of Germany. This had a devastating effect on 'Little Italy', the Italian quarter of Manchester centred on Ancoats, a residential area bordering the city centre. There had been a sizeable number of Italians in Manchester since the latter half of the nineteenth century, when thousands left the farming regions of Italy in search of work. Gradually an Italian colony clustered together and settled in Ancoats. As the cotton industry began to decline the Italians, in order to earn a living, turned to the skills of making ice cream which they had brought from their homeland. Italian ice cream, then as now, proved very popular. The Italians were sociable people and integrated well with their English neighbours. Some married English girls and became British citizens. Numbers of them had served in the Great War with the British forces so it came as a tremendous shock to discover that suddenly they were the enemy. Where before there had been only welcome and friendliness there were now riots against the 'Italian enemies'. Churchill saw them all as a threat to national security and ordered internment of every Italian male aged between 17 and 60. The men were arrested and taken away, leaving their wives and children in tears without any form of support. Some of them even had sons serving in the British army. Despite their protestations of loyalty all Italian men were questioned about their loyalties and if they supported the 'Fascisti'. The answers given appear to have been irrelevant because they were all interned. Most from Manchester were taken to Warth Mill in Bury (a town now part of Greater Manchester). The mill was in poor condition with a leaking roof and little sanitation. There were just twenty toilets and washbasins for up to 2,000 internees. They slept on the floor on straw-filled palliasses. Utensils for eating and drinking were basic. Each internee was given a mess tin with a knife, fork and spoon, and a tin mug. An Italian priest, Monsignor Rossi, interned with them, praised the men for the resourcefulness they showed, despite their predicament, in cooking proper meals, keeping themselves clean and attending religious services. It was consequently decided that several of the Manchester internees should be sent, together with others, to Canada, and the SS *Arandora Star* was commissioned to transport them. Tragically, on 2 July the ship was sunk by a U-boat off the west coast of Ireland. Some 470 Italians, many from Manchester, lost their lives together with a number of

German internees and some of the ship's crew. Any internees who survived were either re-interned in Britain or sent to Australia. Those left at home in Little Italy scarcely fared any better. Ice cream manufacture was banned, although due more to a shortage of ingredients than the fact that it was an Italian industry. Community activities were banned and a curfew was imposed. Rationing was strict and money was scarce. It was a miserable time for all Italians and in addition they had to suffer rampant dislike and distrust from people they had previously considered their friends. Manchester, however, was much kinder to its Italian population than the neighbouring city of Liverpool or other towns and cities in the United Kingdom where there were riots and Italian businesses were attacked and destroyed. Italian women found the disruption and dislocation particularly hard. Not only did they lose their menfolk, but their children were evacuated and many were left feeling totally bereft. It was no easier for the children either. One boy, evacuated with his classmates from St Michael's School in Ancoats to Lytham St Annes near Blackpool, described how Italian children were singled out by the teacher for ridicule. Although Ancoats folk did not show much active hostility towards their Italian neighbours, the community changed. Some Italians left Manchester. The children who remained were disturbed. Some Italians opposed military service while others remained in the Allied forces simply to fight against fascism. Another boy and his sister, both from Gorton, were sent to stay with Italian relatives for the duration for the war, but to the Italians they were foreign. Although they could speak some Italian they were regarded as British. They learned to speak Italian but on their return to Manchester they found it hard to re-adapt. Italian nationality and/or internment resulted in many Mancunian Italians becoming outcasts.

Manchester had internment camps but not within the city and its suburbs. Ideally the internment camps needed to be placed in more isolated areas, away from populations and roads, both of which offered good means of escape. The Isle of Man, a Crown Dependency, was used because escape would be difficult, if not impossible, as it was surrounded by the sea. However, the island is not that large and there were limits as to how many internees it could take. Manchester's internees were predominantly Italian and German. Warth Mill and Burr's Mill in Bury (now a part of Greater Manchester) were used in addition to Stanhill POW camp near Accrington in

Lancashire and Ainsworth/Lowercroft Camp close to Bury and Bolton (both now part of Greater Manchester). The mills were damp but the mostly Italian inmates made the best of it. Warth Mill was used for Italian internees from Little Italy in the Manchester inner suburb of Ancoats. Burr's Mill was used mainly for Italian POWs. Strangely enough these imprisoned soldiers were allowed more freedom than the internees although it is likely that the internees would have been far more loyal to their British neighbours.

Both the Jews and the Italians suffered discrimination during the war, although almost all of them were loyal to Britain, despite efforts to provide evidence to the contrary. However, one group of immigrants in the city not mentioned in accounts of the war were the Chinese. Today Manchester has a thriving and distinctive Chinese quarter with a unique (to Europe) Chinese archway close to the city centre. Chinese food, culture, art and medicine are enjoying great popularity. However, in the 1940s there was no recognizably separate Chinese community. There were around 2,000 individual Chinese people resident in Manchester, most of whom were employed in the traditional laundry trade. After the war, the demand for laundries declined, mainly due to the advent of domestic washing machines. The Chinese adapted by opening restaurants selling Chinese food instead and this provided a basis for the formation of a Chinese community in the city. In any case China was fighting on the side of the Allies during the Second World War and so Chinese citizens were not seen as 'aliens' in the public mind.

By this time the Manchester Regiment (whose headquarters were in Ashton-under-Lyne) was distinguishing itself in the recently-begun land fighting, just as it had done during the dark days of the Great War. There was no doubting the courage and abilities of the 'Manchesters', as they were known, but one member of the Regiment stormed his way into despatches, gossip columns and the history books for his daring and often astonishing feats. Lieutenant-Colonel John Malcolm Thorpe Fleming Churchill was not a Mancunian. He was born in Ceylon and educated on the Isle of Man and at Sandhurst, but he served in the Manchester Regiment from 1926 to 1936 and 1939 to 1959. Throughout the war he fought completely unconventionally, armed with a longbow, bagpipes and a Scottish broadsword. His motto was 'Any officer who goes into action without his sword is improperly dressed'. 'Mad Jack' (as he was known) might be thought to have been born out of his time but his skills in fencing, archery and piping were not in doubt. He had won second place in military piping at the 1938 Aldershot Tattoo and he represented Britain at the World Archery Championships held in Oslo in 1939. He re-joined the Manchester Regiment in September 1939 after the declaration of war. The regiment formed part of the British Expeditionary Force in France, as it had in the Great War, and 'Mad Jack' was sent with his regiment to Dunkirk where a large number of Allied troops had been trapped by the German military on the northern coast of France. Allied commanders had decided on a mass evacuation back across the Channel since that was the only way left to go. To the bemusement of the German forces, although there was considerable loss of Allied lives and equipment, 338,226 soldiers were rescued by 800 boats of every size and description between 26 May and 4 June 1940, resulting in the defeat being ultimately hailed as a victory. 'Mad Jack' was one of the first of the rescue contingent to arrive at Dunkirk. Giving his men the signal to attack the Germans, who were firing on unprotected Allied soldiers waiting on the beaches, he shot a German sergeant with an arrow from his longbow. It was a swift, silent and unexpected way of killing an enemy, he said. The incident also earned him a place in the history books since he was the only British soldier to have killed an enemy with a longbow during the war and the first British soldier since the sixteenth century to use this deadly method of combat. For the rest of the war Jack Churchill served as a Commando, although he remained a member of the Manchester Regiment. He saw action in Norway in 1941 for which he received the Military Cross, and in Sicily in 1943 for which he received the Distinguished Service Medal. He had landed at Salerno with his Scottish broadsword at his waist, his longbow and arrows slung around his neck and his bagpipes under his arm, infiltrating the town of Molina with the help of just one corporal, and capturing a German observation post, a mortar position and forty-two prisoners. His regimental service was a story of which Mancunians were justly proud and 'Fighting Jack Churchill' became part of Manchester military history with honours.

Heaton Park, one of the largest parks in Europe, which lies in the outer Manchester suburb of Blackley, had been used for training 'Pals' Battalions of the Manchester Regiment during the Great War. It was a municipal park of over 600 acres created in 1902, and the eighteenth-century Heaton Hall had been used as a military hospital during the Great War. The Second World War was a very different war and this time Heaton Park was commandeered by the RAF who trained over 133,500 air crew in its grounds. It had its own barrage-balloon site, searchlights and an anti-aircraft gun emplacement, not to mention a swimming pool. Two 'pre-fab' housing estates and a school were built in the Park during the war but these have not survived. The Germans knew perfectly well where Heaton Park was and what its function was. Aerial reconnaissance by the Luftwaffe had resulted in some detailed maps of the place. Heaton Park was bombed three times early in the war. The first attack came at the beginning of June 1940 when high-explosive bombs and a 400lb (181.5kg) incendiary bomb were dropped. This was followed by several high-explosive bombs dropped on 16 September 1940. The third attack came shortly after the Christmas Blitz on Manchester in 1940 when a few high-explosive bombs were dropped near the western perimeter of Heaton Park.

The evacuation of the Channel Islands is one of the defining moments of the Second World War because it represented the first surrender of UK territory to the Germans and remains the only German occupation of UK soil. It was decided that towns and cities in the north-west of England should take the majority of Channel Island evacuees and Manchester was the first official destination. Despite their own difficulties and hardships Manchester folk opened their hearts and their homes to the frightened young evacuees, children far from home, and often their parents and families, relying on total strangers for food, shelter and a little kindness. Ironically many Manchester children had already been evacuated to the country for their safety because Manchester, as an industrial city with a port (via the Manchester Ship Canal), and a large, often densely-packed population, was a prime target for the Luftwaffe. In June 1940, it had been decided to offer evacuation to the people of the Channel Islands as Churchill proposed to leave the islands undefended, due to lack of resources, and the Germans made no secret of their intention to occupy them as soon as possible. Hitler wanted 'a model occupation' on British soil to demonstrate that life under the jackboots (as his troops had become known in reference to their footwear) would not be so bad; it might, in fact, even be quite pleasant. The Channel Islands consist of two 'Bailiwicks' each headed by a Bailiff and governed by an English Lieutenant-Governor. The Bailiwick of Jersey consists of Jersey and a few small 'off-islands'. The Bailiwick of Guernsey consists of Guernsey, Alderney, Herm and Sark. The

Lieutenant-Governors of both bailiwicks left on 21 June, the day of France's surrender to the Germans, leaving the islands to their fate; and to this day many Channel Islanders still feel that they were abandoned to their fate in their hour of need by the United Kingdom.

Alexander Coutanche, the Bailiff of Jersey, was a strong and charismatic man who insisted that there was not much danger to the civilian population of the island and, consequently, only 6,000 of the 50,000 population were evacuated from Jersey as against 17,000 of the 41,000 population from its smaller sister island of Guernsey, and nearly 2,000 from Alderney. The Guernsey Bailiwick was a mixed bag. The Germans intended that the whole island of Alderney would become a troop centre and prison-camp site and it was advised that the island should be completely depopulated. Herm was too small to be taken much notice of by either the Germans or the Guernsiaise. The Dame of Sark, Sybil Hathaway, firmly announced that none of the Sarkese inhabitants would be leaving. Sark was, and still is, an island run on feudal lines, and the tenants of Dame Sybil's little fiefdom were not in any position to defy her authority. Guernsey itself seemed to be in two minds about evacuation, although the local authorities generally advised it, and, in the end, some of the population left and some didn't. A number of those welcoming the evacuees in Manchester were not exactly sure where the Channel Islands were situated and whether or not the islanders spoke English. Most did but an Island patois of English/French was still widely spoken and so occasionally interpreters were needed. Manchester was about as different from Guernsey as it was possible to be. Guernsey is a pretty, rural, sea-girt island whose main industries were farming, fishing and some tourism, to which have been added financial services and the facilities of a tax haven in more recent times. Manchester was a large, dirty, often smog-bound city full of cotton mills, steel and chemical industries, transport and noise. The culture shock must have been dreadful.

Northern folk are kind and caring, however, used to times of hardship and deprivation, sharing whatever they have with others. The Women's Voluntary Service (WVS) and the Salvation Army gave the bewildered evacuees a warm welcome and a good northern tea while they allocated children and families to places where they would stay. Blankets, clothing and food had been collected for everyone while books and toys were given to the children. Manchester, plus Stockport, Marple, Eccles, Oldham and Bury (all towns now within

Clothing depot for refugees in Deansgate, Manchester, 7 January 1941.
(Courtesy of Manchester Central Library Local Studies)

Greater Manchester) took sizeable numbers of Guernsey refugees. No one knew at the time that these children, or the mothers and teachers who had travelled with them, would be separated from the rest of their families for five long years. They could not even write letters home because of the occupation of the Channel Islands. Each town or city had their own billeting officer who would decide where children should be billeted and with whom. Hosts were paid a basic allowance by the government to feed and clothe the evacuee children but this was frequently inadequate and the child's welfare often depended upon the generosity and compassion of their host. Many billets were in rural areas well away from bombing targets. Billeting was compulsory. Although it was mostly a case of using all available space, a number didn't see it that way, some feeling that it was a great imposition. For example, a single person living in a three- or four-bedroom house might be ordered to take three or four children. Another problem was that many of the children came from homes where standards and expectations were different from those of their temporary carers. Others simply had no idea how to look after children. Evacuee children were expected to attend schools in their billeted locality. This caused bullying in some cases and fights broke out. Many children were desperately homesick at first and cried for their parents. It was a difficult situation. However, for the most part, Mancunian folk went out of their way to resolve any initial problems and the majority of children had good experiences. Family members were usually kept together. Although Manchester had been ordered to take the Channel Islands refugees and care for them, the city had no intention of exposing them to attacks from the Luftwaffe when their own children had been sent away for safety. Most evacuees were sent far away from the dangers of the inner city to more outlying towns, like Buxton and Knutsford, while others went to country villages like Cheadle Hulme and Didsbury (which still flies a Guernsey flag on the Channel Islands Liberation Day, 9 May). Many of the evacuees therefore escaped the worst of the German Blitz on Manchester that destroyed much of the city. When the war finally ended not everyone returned home. Some children had grown up, found jobs, even married and had children of their own. Several of the adults who accompanied them had found new jobs or partners and stayed in the UK as well. Commemorative plaques were put up in several towns, Stockport especially, in recognition and memory of all the evacuees and similar plaques were also erected in the Channel Islands. Not every evacuee's story had a happy ending, but the majority did, and lasting friendships were formed. Manchester was justly proud of the part the city had played in hosting and caring for so many Channel Islands children despite the savage destruction of many parts of the city by German bombers. London, Birmingham, Liverpool, Sheffield, Bristol, Southampton and Coventry had also suffered badly in the heavy German bombing campaigns as well as Manchester, so it was a shock when, shortly after the sixty-fifth anniversary of the end of the war and the liberation of the Channel Islands, a few folk in the Bailiwick of Guernsey posted on social networks that England hadn't really suffered much, if at all, at German hands in the Second World War. Their motive was, and is, unknown, but there is still bitterness about the belief that the Channel Islands were abandoned by the British in 1940. That is another story but it does not alter or denigrate the contribution made by Manchester in caring for the Channel Islands evacuees and in giving them as safe and decent a life as possible. Links between Jersey, Guernsey and the towns and cities of

Northern England remain strong and the ties of living memory will ensure they remain so for the foreseeable future.

However, the Channel Islands refugees generally fared better than Jewish refugees. At least partly due to the efforts of Oswald Mosley with his Blackshirts and the BUF some anti-Semitic feeling had been expressed in Manchester against its own Jewish population (an anti-Semitism which finally erupted into post-war riots at Cheetham Hill in 1947). Some German- and Austrian-born Jews were interned at Warth Mill along with the Italians where they found the conditions just as basic and difficult. There was often a certain caution about admitting Jewish refugees due to fear of creating 'a backlash against alien foreigners', in other words fuelling anti-Semitism. Despite its sizeable Jewish population, Manchester, like many other towns and cities, took a share of Jewish refugees, especially after Kristallnacht in November 1938 when the Nazi hatred of Jews in Germany exploded into bloody violence. They were offered shelter by the Manchester Rotary Club in hostels as well as in the homes of Jewish folk already living in the city. The Lancashire Development Company offered them some employment, but Jewish folk were also keen to do their bit for the war effort, working on the home front and in local industries, joining the armed forces and the Women's Land Army. However, the British authorities sometimes found it necessary to limit the number of Jewish refugees, which split families, often leaving many to their fate at the hands of the Nazis. Sometimes it was a simple question of economics, with many Jewish families on the Continent only being able to afford to send their children to safety, while the adults remained in their homes until most of them were sent to the concentration camps. One such child, a Jewish girl in her early teens, had arrived in Manchester on her own in the late 1930s. She was kindly treated by her Mancunian hosts, but she subsequently learned that her whole family had been murdered by the Nazis. Her grief and shock were overwhelming and she never really recovered. She was an attractive girl, vivacious, but also volatile as a result of her family's tragedy. Although she later married a Mancunian, and had two children of her own, she could never come to terms with what had happened to her family in the war, and she slowly lost her mind, finally dying long before her time in a Manchester sanatorium. She was a close friend of this writer's mother but her details have been given anonymously to spare further grief for her children. It was just one of many such tragedies.

For Manchester, as for most towns and cities in Britain, life was rapidly becoming harder. Income tax rose again and an additional tax was also placed on tobacco, but the measure which drew the loudest squeals of discontent was an increase in postage costs because that directly affected letters to troops serving abroad. Purchase tax was also introduced in October at 33.3 per cent on luxury goods. Its aim was to reduce perceived wastage of raw materials on non-essential luxuries. A Limitation of Supplies Order had been passed in June reducing seventeen classes of non-essential consumer goods to two-thirds of their pre-war production. These included toys, jewellery, cutlery and pottery. Black-market goods, sold by profiteers, still flourished, which caused huge resentment amongst many people. Learning from the lessons of the Great War, an amendment was added in July to the new and more stringent Emergency Powers (Defence) Act 1940, passed in May 1940, banning strikes for the duration of the war and forcing compulsory arbitration in disputes. Strike action during the Great War had disrupted the unity of the Home Front and incensed members of the armed forces serving away from home. Churchill did not want internal strife adding to the problems caused by another costly war which had to be funded somehow. There was also a need to reduce imports and return to the frugal years of make do and mend austerity which had characterized the Great War. Winston Churchill had served under David Lloyd George during the Great War and he was quick to see the benefits of Lloyd George's ideas on self-sufficiency in wartime. Lloyd George, now 77, was frail and ill, although still an MP. Churchill, however, was firmly in command. It was 'his time'. He had been quick to re-introduce food rationing, bacon, sugar, tea, butter and meat being among the first foods to be rationed. Jam, cereals, biscuits, cheese, eggs, lard, milk, and canned and dried fruit were quick to follow. Although in several respects rationing in the Second World War was more severe than in the Great War, it fulfilled the intention of keeping the population healthy and fed, if not well fed. The amount of meat was halved and one egg, instead of four, was all that was allowed per person per week, but, unlike the Great War, bread and vegetables were not rationed. People complained about the 'war bread' as they had done in the Great War but the main cause of dissatisfaction seemed to be that the bread was brown and not white. A Manchester lad who had been evacuated from the city, but returned after leaving school in the summer of 1940, lamented that bread was no longer home-baked and

Weekly rations	
First World War	Second World War
2oz tea [approx. 16 tea bags]	2oz tea
8oz sugar	8oz sugar
4 pints milk	2 pints + 1 pint of dried milk
1 loaf [large brown]	Not rationed
4oz butter	2oz butter + 2oz margarine
4oz cheese	4oz cheese
4 eggs	1 egg + 3 dried eggs in powder form
2oz bacon	4oz bacon and ham
2lb meat	12oz meat
1lb porridge oats	Not rationed
5lbs potatoes	Not rationed
1lb carrots	Not rationed
1lb onions [white]	Not rationed
2lbs green vegetables	Not rationed
1lb fruit	Not rationed
½lb rice	Rationed as 8/24 monthly food points
1 small jar of preserves	4oz jam

Note: 1oz = just over 28g; 1lb = approx. 454g

he also mourned the passing of pigeon pies. Chips, jam butties (sandwiches for the benefit of readers living in the south of the country) and beans on toast now seemed to form a considerable part of the staple diet in the poorer suburbs.

Shopping during the war was different to that of today. There were no food, cleaning materials, toiletries, or household items in all-under-one-roof supermarkets. Grocery shopping relied on individual shops and customers tended to patronise their own regular suppliers so that strangers coming into a shop might not receive the same quality or quantity of certain goods. Although potatoes were not rationed some greengrocers would only sell 1lb (just under 500g) to a customer whom they had not seen before. Manchester communities and suburbs were still quite tightly-knit and local shopkeepers could immediately recognize someone not from those parts. It was hard on customers if they were not known but it did prevent better off shoppers going to different districts and buying up foods to hoard or sell on for a profit. Meat was bought from the butchers, fish from the fishmongers, bread from the bakery, fruit and vegetables from the greengrocers, tins, preserves and dried goods etc. from the general grocery stores, and newspapers and tobacco from the newsagent. There was no automation or self-service. Each customer was served individually by a shop assistant, so shopping took much longer, and when shopkeepers were dealing with ration books and coupons and limited stocks of commodities, long queues formed. One schoolboy said he didn't so much queue as shove because often most things had sold out by the time the last in the queue had reached the counter. The length of the queues were of concern to both local civic authorities and national government due to the time involved and the disruption they could cause.

Merchant shipping was being constantly attacked and was suffering heavy losses. Churchill, like Lloyd George had done in the Great War, actively promoted self-sufficiency and the slogan 'Dig for Victory' was once more employed. Local newspapers published gardening tips but the Ministry of Agriculture issued a series of Dig for Victory leaflets. The first one included a table of planting for vegetables. There were four columns headed 'Crop', Time of Sowing', 'Distance Apart' subdivided into rows and plants, and, finally, 'Period for Use'. It was designed to allow folk to supply themselves and their neighbours with fresh vegetables all year round. A big part of the Dig for Victory campaign was to grow produce for winter as well as for summer. British-grown winter vegetables are mostly limited to carrots, onions, potatoes, cabbage, kale and sprouts. The choice of fruit was basically apples or pears. Most ordinary folk did not have refrigerators, still less freezers, so bottling, preserving and pickling was popular and encouraged. Most housewives still made their own jams and chutneys if they could do so. Apple, tomato and onion chutneys were favoured rather than more exotic types. Sweet and savoury jelly spreads, such as redcurrant or mint, were also well liked. Eating patterns were different as well. Many ordinary folk had either porridge or bread and jam for breakfast. Partly due to rationing, but also partly due to custom, snacking between meals was discouraged or even forbidden in some cases. The midday meal (then called dinner in the North and lunch in the South) was the main meal of meat and vegetables with a pudding of some description. Tea was slices of bread and jam or dripping (meat juices from the pan) and a mug of tea, with perhaps a slice of some plain cake.

The farmers were not having an easy time as the imports of Spanish potash fertilisers had practically ceased. Before the war Spanish potash had provided much of the fertiliser used by farmers. Alternative potash deposits in Alsace, which had also been used, were now in the hands of the enemy. As in the Great War, public parks and open spaces were again set aside for individuals to grow fruit and vegetables as well as private gardens and some farming land. Piccadilly, in the centre of Manchester, which today houses the bus station, No. 1 Piccadilly and an ugly concrete wall, was simply a collective block of allotments during the war. Folk living in central Manchester did not possess gardens as a rule and open public spaces like Piccadilly were divided into allotments. Women bore the main brunt of the quest for economy and conservation of food supplies. Many worked on the allotments but it was their role in the kitchen which was most important. A leaflet entitled 'Women and the Home Front' openly exhorted women to refrain from hoarding or encouraging profiteering and to take pride in daily thrift because, said the leaflet, '... in this spirit, we can fight to conquer ... the greed and selfishness which are the ultimate causes of war itself ...'. Wartime recipes centre heavily on fresh fruit and vegetables and non-meat main dishes were popular. A variation on the modern Quiche Lorraine was a flan of potatoes, onions, celery and a little cheese mixed in a white sauce and baked in a pastry flan case. Offal was a much more popular form of meat. Many folk today recoil at the thought of eating liver or kidneys, and the mere mention of sweetbreads (the throat or pancreas of calf or lamb) and tripe (the stomach lining from a sheep or cow) with onions would be enough to send most youngsters straight to the nearest McDonalds. Rice puddings, made with water (the taste is indistinguishable from those made with milk) were very popular and so were suet-based puddings like jam roly-poly or spotted dick. The water from boiled cabbages was said to make a refreshing drink. Fish and chip shops were popular, although fish was often in short supply and expensive. Beef dripping was sometimes used to fry chips which gave them an excellent taste, but more often than not it was low-quality cooking fat. Churchill was also very keen on Lloyd George's idea of national kitchens. These had proved a great success in the First World War and the idea was revived early in 1940. Initially they were called community kitchens until Churchill re-named them British Kitchens or Restaurants. The concept was just the same as in the Great War. The kitchens could bulk-buy fresh foods at cost and cook

Allotments at Piccadilly, Manchester, 20 July 1942.
(*Courtesy of Manchester Central Library Local Studies*)

cheap nourishing meals on a small number of industrial cookers. This saved both money on individual food purchases and fuel for running individual cookers. Each kitchen had a restaurant attached which was decently furnished. There were cloths on the tables, sometimes a vase of flowers, and the ambience was cosy and sociable. Customers could buy a meat-and-two-vegetables main course followed by a pudding for the modern equivalent of £1. Meals would be simple but quite palatable. Spam with mashed potato, hotpot, stew, pie and mash, baked potatoes, curry (of anything – curried carrots were a favoured dish) and rice, greens in season, with maybe a rice or suet pudding to follow. Horsemeat was also used and there was a horse-meat butchers in Gorton. Although horses had been prized and necessary in the Great War, this war was a very different one and cavalry was not used. Sometimes there might be a soup as well, usually a thin vegetable soup, not the thick soups folk have become used to today. These restaurants were not soup kitchens nor charity projects. They were designed to protect people's self-respect but they had to make a profit which was then put towards either food supplies or opening more restaurants. Manchester had a number of British Restaurants which proved ideal for those working long hours, busy mothers trying to be both breadwinners and homemakers as well as caring for their children, and those who were finding life a serious struggle. The whole of the North-West had seventy-four of these restaurants in 1941, each catering for an area of nearly 58,000 people (by 1943 this number had risen to 166).

The war had affected all the main Manchester hospitals which needed to provide for additional facilities and responsibilities. Manchester Royal Infirmary spent £3,000 (£143,800 today) on air-raid precautions at the Infirmary and its convalescent home and the provision of additional supplies as a reserve for war emergencies. Christies increased its hospital supplies and 'fitted up a laboratory in a radon cave' for treating its patients. St Mary's Hospital for Women and Children introduced several new schemes for the treatment of patients and the reorganization put a severe strain on hospital finances. Manchester Royal Eye Hospital, which also took patients from the Midlands and other areas of Northern England, had recently been enlarged and increased its equipment to deal with the 120,000 patients seen each year, hoping that this would be adequate to deal with wartime injuries as well. Ancoats Hospital passed a resolution appealing for funds to build a new out-patients department on recently acquired land. The Dental Hospital had recently opened new dental facilities for treating patients but was also in desperate need of extra income.

Manchester held a War Weapons Week in mid-October with the aim of raising £10,000,000 (£479,500,000 today) to facilitate the purchase of a battleship for the fight against Hitler. On the first day £3,053,000 (£146,400,000) was raised, much to everyone's delight. A naval contingent of 300 men and a full gun crew arrived from a

'The time has come to stand together...' Manchester University, 1940.

training base in the North-West, marching through the streets of the city accompanied by the band of the Royal Marines and assisting with collections for the fund. Manchester Corporation gave £500,000 (£23,970,000) while the Refuge Assurance Company, the Co-operative Insurance Society Limited, and the local banks each gave £250,000 (£11,990,000). The British Cotton Growers Association donated £100,000 (£4,795,000) and Manchester Victoria University gave £10,000 (£479,500). War Bonds also did well from small private donations and folk in the streets showered a display wagon travelling around the city centre with silver and copper which raised another £12 (£575). On the second day of the week an RAF band visited the city, marching from London Road Station (now Piccadilly) via Whitworth Street, Oxford Street, Peter Street, Deansgate, St Mary's Gate and Market Street to Piccadilly Gardens, where the band played for half an hour before returning to London Road once more via Portland Street, Oxford Street, Mosley Street and Piccadilly.

On 10 July the Battle of Britain began. It lasted three months and three weeks until Hallowe'en that year. 'Never has so much been owed by so many to so few' said Winston Churchill proudly after the brave young pilots of the RAF had established supremacy over the Luftwaffe and gained control of the skies. The battle took place mainly in the skies over Southern England and East Anglia; although

Bomb damage at the Royal Exchange in Manchester, 24 December 1940.
(Courtesy of Manchester Central Library Local Studies)

the whole of the east coast was vulnerable. Manchester, on the western side of the country, was not involved in the aerial dogfights, but the city had large industrial complexes in addition to the Avro and Vickers aircraft factories which turned out Spitfires and later Lancaster bombers. The Germans had decided on a policy of fighting the RAF by day and bombing industrial centres at night. Consequently, air raids on Manchester began on 8 August 1940. Along with the incendiary bombs the Germans also dropped a bundle of leaflets, with 'Hitler's last appeal to reason' emblazoned across the front. The bundle was clearly intended to split open on impact and the wind would then distribute the leaflets. This did not happen. The bundle did not open and struck a policeman instead. He was not badly hurt and no doubt put the leaflets to what he considered to be a suitable use. The first bombs caused little damage but on 29 August a bomb hit the gas main in Hulme which caused a large fire and there were further incendiaries dropped on Moss Side and Rusholme, followed the next day by hits on Knott Mill in Ardwick, the College of Technology and, in early September, Didsbury, Northenden, Withington and Chorlton-cum-Hardy were all attacked. There were intermittent raids throughout the autumn, and firewatchers were kept busy, but these initial attacks had taken Manchester a little unawares. Air-raid sirens, hooters or whistles which gave out short blasts or a continuous whining noise, often alternating every few seconds, had first sounded in the city towards the end of June but that had been a false alarm, and the sense of security caused by the 'Phoney War' had remained to some extent undisturbed until the end of August. The sirens would sound when enemy aircraft were approaching and then again when the aircraft were directly overhead. Most people would run for the shelters when the first alarm sounded but those engaged on war work had to wait until the second round of sirens sounded with the consequence that death or injury was much more common for these workers. The 'all clear' signal was given by the sirens sounding continuously for two minutes. Air-raid shelters, barrage balloons and firewatching were the main forms of defence adopted in addition to brilliant searchlights aimed at enemy aircraft so that anti-aircraft guns (known as 'ack-acks') on the ground could fire accurately to try and bring down their prey. There were several anti-aircraft gun positions in and around Manchester including one at Broadhurst Park in Moston, one near Kingsway Park for defending the Trafford industrial complex, and those in Heaton Park, with accompanying aerial search lights. Sometimes lorries towed the 'ack-ack' guns around, stopping in different locations and firing, to give the Germans the impression that there were more anti-aircraft gun emplacements than there actually were. Barrage balloons, large oval silver-grey balloons, sometimes known as 'blimps', tethered by metal cables, were used to try and force aircraft to fly at higher altitudes, thereby making their approach more difficult and making it harder to hit intended targets. The balloons were often deployed and maintained by members of the WAAF and a Mancunian lady named Irene Forsdyke was one of those chosen to work on the barrage balloons protecting Manchester. As she and her colleagues discovered, it was a task that needed careful concentration, conscientiousness and courage, plus a good deal of technical knowledge. Ten weeks training was required and the women needed to understand the meaning of teamwork because this was essential if there were any serious problems with the balloons or there were adverse weather conditions. The balloons had a standard 90ft (27.5m) 'circle' and a winch powered by a Ford V8 engine to raise and lower the balloon. The last few feet of the cable drum were painted red in warning because if the metal cable ran off the drum the balloon would be loose and the operator was in danger of being decapitated.

Maximum ceiling was 5,000ft (1,524m) but most were flown at 500ft (152.5m). Each balloon was attached by rigging and a 'tail guy' anchored to its circle by a 'free-running fly wheel'. If the wind changed this had to be changed. The balloons were filled with hydrogen and required daily maintenance. Some of the male military commanders were not happy at first about women being employed to carry out this work but had to admit that the WAAF members handled the task well. Dame Laura Knight, a Derbyshire-born war artist, was commissioned by the War Artist's Advisory Committee to paint a balloon site with WAAFs at work to encourage recruitment of more women for the purpose. However, barrage balloons were largely ineffective against the high-level bombers with which the Germans replaced their low-level dive bombers after considerable success by the RAF in shooting them down. London had the largest number of defensive barrage balloons but Manchester had several as well.

Barrage balloon in a Manchester park, 18 June 1941.
(Courtesy of Manchester Central Library Local Studies)

Firewatching was done by civil defence volunteers. The tallest buildings had small shelters which could accommodate firewatchers and their job was to see where the incendiary bombs fell, then take appropriate action. Single 'incendiary magnesium electron' bombs could be smothered in a bucket of sand. Small fires were put out with buckets of water but the fire service had to be notified immediately of larger fires. This writer's mother was a firewatcher during the war. She worked as a teacher in an infants' school at Ardwick in Manchester during the day but at night she had rostered firewatching duties in the neighbouring town of Stockport (now part of Greater Manchester) where she lived. Often lonely, cold and scared, she would watch the bombs dropping and desperately pray that they would not hit the building where she was doing firewatching duty. She was one of the lucky ones. It was dangerous work and a number of firewatchers lost their lives.

It was quickly realized that air-raid shelters built at ground level did not offer much protection and that it was safer to be underground. In the Spanish Civil War, Barcelona, which had become a Republican (freedom fighters) stronghold, suffered heavy bombing by the Germans and the Italians. The city suffered 194 aerial attacks which destroyed 1,500 buildings and killed 2,500 people. The Spanish people have a very creative streak and it was in Barcelona that the first underground bomb-proof shelters were built. These initial shelters were built as a network of tunnels cut into the native bedrock. They were fitted with benches, toilets, electric lighting run from batteries and first-aid facilities. Several British engineers visited Barcelona to study the effects of bombing and the construction of the underground shelters. One, a scientist named J.B.S. Haldane, wrote:

> There were four entrances which led down by ramps with a few steps to the tunnels. The ramps twisted repeatedly, until a depth of about 55 feet below the ground was reached. Here began a labyrinth of passages about 7 feet high by 4 feet broad. They were cut in the very tough soil of the district, and had no lining, and I think no supports such as pit props. They were, however, being lined with tiles with a cement backing so as to give a semi-circular arch and vertical walls.

The idea of using tunnels as air-raid shelters caught on quickly after the commencement of hostilities and Manchester had a number of existing tunnels which proved ideal for the purpose. However, they were not within the reach of everyone and the idea of more simple and economic underground shelters evolved. One of the most popular shelters was the Anderson shelter, named after its designer, Sir John Anderson. These measured 6ft 6in (1.95m) by 4ft 6in (1.35m) and were made from six curved corrugated-iron sheets bolted together, which were then half buried in the earth in people's gardens. The entrance would be protected by 'a steel shield and an earthen blast wall'. However, many people in Manchester did not have a garden and for them the alternative was the Morrison shelter, designed by John Baker and named after the Home Secretary of the day, Herbert Morrison. This was rather like a big steel dog cage measuring 6ft (2m) long by 4ft (1.2m) wide by 2ft 6in (0.75m) high. It was placed in a downstairs room, often the kitchen, where the top could be used as a table. A mattress was usually put inside for comfort and people sheltered there during raids since it could supposedly withstand tons of falling rubble.

Morrison air-raid shelter, Manchester, 19 February 1941.
(Courtesy of Manchester Central Library Local Studies)

Some houses had basements and cellars but it rapidly became obvious as the war progressed that deeper underground shelters were more effective (the London Underground railway tunnels were famously used). Manchester did not have an underground railway system but the city did have tunnels, vaults, cellars and basements beneath the city, mostly built by Victorian engineers for storage, maintenance, canal passage and culverting the now-lost River Tib. Manchester Town Hall has a large basement which was used for war rooms. The John Rylands library on Deansgate has extensive storage vaults below ground, and Deansgate in fact had its own air-raid shelter beneath the Great Northern Railway Company's goods warehouse which survived the Blitz and stands on the corner of Deansgate and Peter Street. The shelters, still lying beneath the modern cinema and restaurants which fill the warehouse today, are no longer accessible to anyone except maintenance engineers.

Some of the city's churches had crypts. Just below the Cathedral, Hunts Bank was widened in the 1830s by the construction of an embankment to improve traffic flow and renamed Victoria Street. The new embankment, built along the Manchester shore of the River Irwell, was supported by seventeen arches (known as the Cathedral Steps or Victoria Arches) which housed various businesses and were

Great Northern Railway Warehouse on corner of Peter Street and Deansgate. Built over the Manchester and Salford Canal, its tunnels were used as air-raid shelters during the war.

Victoria Arches below Manchester Cathedral, the site of former air-raid shelters.

also used as landing stages for boat trips along the Irwell, the river that separates Manchester from its sister city of Salford. Early in the war these arches were converted into air-raid shelters designed to accommodate just over 1,600 people, and included a medical station, kitchen and toilet facilities. The extensive toilets, used after the war as public toilets, were not closed until 1967. They were all that then remained of the wartime features, but public tours of the former shelters were organized on a regular basis. However, a few years ago, the Irwell flooded and the water rose to the ceilings of the old shelters and toilets. After the floods receded it was decided that there were too many health and safety issues to allow public access, although engineers and the occasional television crew are sometimes permitted to go down to what are now the 'damp, dark, dank, depths' (eye-witness description). Externally, the bricked-up archways can still be seen in the retaining wall on the Manchester side of the Irwell.

In addition, there were tunnels beneath the old fire station and the former Ancoats hospital, as well a disused tunnel of the Manchester and Salford Junction Canal, part of which ran beneath the Great Northern Railway Company Warehouse on the corner of Deansgate and Peter Street. All these tunnels were used as air-raid shelters; although there is no longer any public access to any of them. The canal tunnel was divided into sixteen sections (bays 1–5 lie beneath Deansgate and the railway warehouse), each individually reinforced, and there were five entry points, in Grape Street, Lower Byrom

Street, Byrom Street, Deansgate, and Watson Street. The shelter had a total capacity of 1,350, but was often used by less than half that number. Facilities included wooden benches, first aid posts and chemical toilets. There were also air-raid shelters beneath the station approach to Manchester Piccadilly designed to hold 1,275 people. There would have been basic sanitation, first aid posts and facilities for making hot drinks and sandwiches, but any surviving features are in areas blocked to public access, although many of the fine vaulted arches of the former shelters soar high above a currently open area used as a car park by day and at weekends for popular musical events organized by the Warehouse Project. Access on foot is gained through swing doors from the Ashton and Etihad Campus tram platform. Gorton had its own air-raid shelters on Gorton Road. However, the best-known air-raid shelters were in Stockport (now part of Greater Manchester), just over 6 miles from Manchester city centre, and they were used by folk from Manchester, Lancashire and Cheshire. Dug deep into the red sandstone cliffs of the Mersey they could accommodate up to 6,500 people and had all modern conveniences such as flushing toilets, medical facilities and kitchens. The insulating properties of earth and rock offered a near-constant temperature, although the lack of windows could be claustrophobic and reliable lighting was essential since complete darkness can induce panic and total disorientation. Nevertheless, this strange, quiet, subterranean world offered shelter and safety in much the same way as the catacombs of Paris did, except that Mancunians only had to share their shelters with the living and not the dead.

The tunnel shelters were at least generally dry with a fairly even temperature. Like the citizens of Barcelona, many Mancunians found the shelters, especially their own small Anderson shelters, claustrophobic, but they tried to make the best of the situation. Mothers took their knitting or sewing with them, children took their favourite toys, and at Christmastime the shelters were decorated with paper chains and sometimes small Christmas trees. The larger tunnel shelters had kitchens which could supply sandwiches and hot drinks, and some of the Anderson shelters had small stoves. There was some fire risk but the danger outside the shelters was far greater. Many people slept in their Anderson shelters every night rather than sleep in their houses with one ear open for the noise of the bombers. The downside of the Anderson shelters was that they were cramped and often cold and

Air-raid shelter beneath Manchester Piccadilly railway station, used today as a car park and for holding musical events.

Bomb damage at the Palace Theatre Manchester, 1940.
(Courtesy of Manchester Central Library Local Studies)

damp. Those who had Morrison shelters often slept in them as well. There was little room in a Morrison shelter for anything except a mattress and a blanket, and they were even more claustrophobic, but, as they could withstand the weight of the rubble caused by a house collapsing, this was a good enough reason to put up with the discomfort. Those who had houses with cellars were a little better off. Cellars offered a ready-made shelter completely below ground, some with two or three rooms. Many of the smaller Manchester houses had single-room cellars or coal cellars, while some of the larger houses had kitchens and laundries in their basements where the cook and housemaid were expected to live as well. They were not as deep as tunnel shelters but they were much safer than remaining on the surface or in shelters unprotected by earth and rocks. Cellars would be furnished and provided with means of making hot drinks and simple meals. Toilet facilities could be primitive, often consisting of little more than a chamber pot or a bucket, and slops would have to be emptied each morning. Nevertheless, most felt it was a small price to pay for escaping death or serious injury.

In October, the Palace Theatre on Oxford Road was bombed and damaged but the worst was yet to come. The Germans chose Christmas 1940 to try and bomb the heart out of Manchester and this caught citizens unprepared to some extent. Family Christmas parties had been planned. There was a Christmas circus at Belle Vue; Tommy Trinder was playing in *Cinderella* at the Opera House and Stanley Holloway was starring in *Robinson Crusoe* at the Palace Theatre. There was official unease that the 'Phoney War' had resulted in evacuated children returning to Manchester because there seemed to be no real danger and the public had generally ignored pleas to reverse this trend.

Hitler's policy of Blitzkreig, German for 'lightning war', was based on speed, surprise, co-ordination and rapid mass attacks on an area to cause maximum destruction, damage to infrastructure, chaos and panic. The Germans knew that Manchester was a major industrial city and that aircraft engines were manufactured in the city. Radio messages had been intercepted that an attack on Manchester was imminent although no one knew exactly when this would happen; but then, on two consecutive nights, just before Christmas Eve 1940, Manchester was attacked repeatedly and mercilessly. Although the city had experienced its first air raid in August 1940 it was not

Bomb damage in the Market Place, Manchester, 24 December 1940.
(*Courtesy of Manchester Central Library Local Studies*)

prepared for the unrelenting and merciless savagery of the 'Blitz' as it became known. Liverpool had been attacked on the night of 21 December and Manchester firefighters, ARP and anti-aircraft gun personnel were alerted. Nothing happened but the following night, the 22nd, literally all hell seemed to break loose. The sirens sounded but the bombers, using the fires still burning in Liverpool to guide them in, struck within minutes. Almost 10,000 incendiary bombs fell in the area around Albert Square within thirty-eight minutes. German bombers followed up by spending three hours dropping an assortment of flares, incendiaries and high explosives to light up and then destroy the area. It must have been terrifying to hear the drone of the aeroplane engines in the dark of the blackout, then to see the skies full of sinister black silhouettes dropping endless destruction upon the city. In total 272 tons of high explosives and 37,000 incendiaries rained down on the city centre. Princess Street, Clarence Street, Deansgate, the Royal Exchange, the Victoria, and the gas main at St Mary's Gate, were all on fire; so too were warehouses on Portland Street, Sackville Street and Watson Street. Grey Street, Stafford Street, Cooke Street and Erskine Street were practically demolished. A part of Manchester's firefighting force was still in Liverpool, helping to tackle the fires there and at first the city burned helplessly. Manchester put out a desperate call for help and firefighters from as far afield as Teeside and London answered the call; but, just when they thought things could not get any worse, the Luftwaffe returned on the night of 23 December and this time they dropped 195 tons of explosives, including some of their largest bombs, the LM1000 parachute mines. This time Manchester citizens knew they were coming because Lord Haw Haw had gleefully broadcast the news as he gloated over the death and destruction the first raid had caused. Most of the city centre was in flames. Folk ran desperately for the air-raid shelters to escape the relentless bombardment. So too did the rats. Those fleeing told of streets littered with hundreds of rats deserting the basements, cellars and hidden corners of buildings where they lived which had been set alight. The air-raid shelters, however, could not always guarantee safety. Gibson's shelter, which was part of Hulme town hall, suffered a direct hit. Although it was only designed to hold 200 people, it was sheltering 450 folk that night. Miraculously no-one was killed and all were rescued successfully. The city was like a nightmare recreation of Dante's Inferno. In total 165 warehouses, 150 offices, five banks, and 250 business premises were destroyed,

Bomb damage in Manchester city centre, 24 December 1940.
(Courtesy of Manchester Central Library Local Studies)

along with 30,000 houses and 100 schools in the area, some of which is now subsumed within Greater Manchester. Over 5,000 people were homeless. In the city 363 people died and, it was said over 1,000 were badly injured in the inner and outer suburbs, and those areas now within Greater Manchester. The city remained lit up in a mass of flame. The Royal Exchange had suffered a direct hit and so too did the Cathedral. Half of Piccadilly was destroyed.

Trafford Park was badly damaged, including the Metropolitan-Vickers aircraft works, Manchester United's football ground was wrecked and in the Shambles only Wellington's Inn and Sinclair's Oyster Bar survived. Deansgate and Oxford Road were severely affected and Exchange railway station was left a smoking ruin. As the fires burned fiercely, dark windowless shells of buildings were starkly outlined in the flames before crumbling and falling as supports gave way under the intense heat. The tragedies were endless. In Miles Platting, a small inner suburb of Manchester, over twenty people from the same family were killed while enjoying a Christmas party

Bomb damage in Hulme, Manchester, 24 December 1940.
(*Courtesy of Manchester Central Library Local Studies*)

together. Three young families, including a number of small children, who lived in Moss Side were also killed. A wedding party at the Manley Arms pub in Clopton Street, Hulme, were killed by a direct hit as well.

Five children were among the fifteen dead in Beswick close to what is now the Etihad Stadium (the present home of Manchester City Football Club). People were killed as far out from the city centre as Moston and Northenden. Total casualties eventually included 684 dead, although this might actually have been as high as 820, and 2,000 injured. It must have seemed like the Apocalypse to bewildered, frightened citizens desperately searching for loved ones in the rubble as bombs rained down and the sky was lit up a fiery red by burning buildings. One girl, shopping in Ancoats when the Luftwaffe struck, said, ' ... the sky was all orange and yellow, it looked like the fireworks I'd seen at Belle Vue ...'. Manchester was stunned. The painting depicting the bombing of Guernica had been no exaggeration. Dr Garfield Williams, the Dean of Manchester Cathedral, wrote that

I have always thought of Manchester Cathedral ... as a lovely jewel set in the midst of the most appalling and disgracefully unworthy surroundings ... but that night the cathedral ... was a

Bomb damage at Manchester Cathedral, 1940.
(*Courtesy of Manchester Central Library Local Studies*)

thing of entrancing, shocking, devastating beauty ... the wind was filled with sparks so as to give the effect of golden rain ... the stained glass windows of the cathedral were all lit up ... to produce a colour effect which was sublime ... the old church a fairy-like scintillating thing ...

The bomb blast had lifted the whole lead roof of the Cathedral before dropping it back into place again! All the doors and windows were gone. Chairs, ornaments, carpets and furnishings lay in tattered heaps. The High Altar and the organ were heaps of rubble. The Lady Chapel, the Ely Chapel and the Regimental Chapel were destroyed; yet the solidity of the old cathedral structure had withstood the bombing. Some saw it as a sign.

At best, folk looking forward to Christmas had simply lost a few presents and maybe a Christmas tree. Many had lost their homes. Some had lost their families. A sizeable number lost their lives. More suffered life-changing injuries. There was a huge sense of shock, tears, grief, anger and bewilderment. The feelings of the citizens can best be summed up in the words of a Surrey housewife who kept a diary of the war years. In August 1940, during the Battle of Britain, she had written '... the atmosphere of the world is poisoned, there is some-thing wrong with [even] the happiest moments ...'. The noise of the fires was so loud that by the time the last bomb was dropped, at 6.00am on Christmas Eve, the engines of the planes could no longer be heard. There was simply, according to eye witnesses, a 'sensation ... just like an earthquake ...' as the bombs hit their targets. Manchester Royal Infirmary had escaped the worst of the holocaust but the nurses' home was badly damaged. The hospital was swamped with casualties from the bombing. They were graded into those need-ing immediate treatment and those requiring medical assessment. The latter group were laid on stretchers or mattresses on the floor to await attention. The electricity supply had been disrupted and many of the windows were boarded up so the nurses worked by the light of hurricane lamps. Outside the fires still raged and there were several explosions. During the day an incendiary bomb fell down a chimney and set one of the wards on fire. The fire was quickly extinguished by a nurse who covered it with sand while her colleagues covered the patients to protect them from dust and soot.

One of the iconic slogans of the war was 'Keep calm and carry on' which is exactly what the citizens of Manchester amazingly managed

Victoria Station in Manchester after the Blitz, 24 December 1940.
(Courtesy of Manchester Central Library Local Studies)

to do. A common response to the shock and fright of the air raids was to desperately want a nice hot sweet cup of tea which were provided in their thousands across the city by nurses, kind-hearted neighbours, and the WVS. In the city, the hospital kitchens had gas cookers and despite everything the kitchen staff managed to cook and serve Christmas lunch the day after the mass destruction caused by the Blitz. Nurses sang carols to the patients who were also given lots of little Christmas teatime treats. The Christmas Blitz drove everything else from Mancunians' minds, yet calmly, without panic or the benefit of bereavement facilities and counselling, they simply concentrated on rescuing survivors, finding food and shelter for those who had escaped, restoring services and trying to clear some of the devastation.

A reporter from the *Manchester City News*, wandering desolately through the ruins of the city, wrote in his newspaper:

> ... As I gazed at the destruction wrought by the filthy hands of precocious murderers, I realized something ... I knew that I loved Manchester ... its dear smoky streets ... its kindly

King George VI inspecting the air-raid damage in Manchester in 1941.
(Courtesy of Manchester Central Library Local Studies)

comradely folk ... the very nooks and alleys of it ... then something in my heart ... said this not Manchester ... .this is a ...
transient outer shell ... Manchester is not a congeries of buildings ... it is built in the line of its citizens ... and that is un-
quenched ... its courage and resolve unextinguishable, high in
aloof pride above Hitler's hatred ... if this be the Battle of
Manchester then Hitler has lost it ...

The Town Hall, the Central Library and the Midland Hotel had
escaped unscathed because, it was rumoured, Hitler had chosen the
latter as his future headquarters in the city. He thought the building
resembled a mediaeval castle and as such would be appropriate,
probably not realizing that the now-lost River Tib runs beneath the
hotel which would have made him vulnerable to surprise attacks. So
much of Manchester had been left burning after the Blitz that the
Germans believed it had been totally destroyed. However, that was
far from the truth and the Germans had made a big mistake if they

The Midland Hotel which Hitler is said to have wanted to make his headquarters.

Winston Churchill in Blitz-damaged Manchester.

thought that these attacks would crush Manchester. A sense of humour and a strong camaraderie united the folk of the city and they took to referring to Manchester as a place that 'Adolf had knocked about a bit ...'. It simply hardened the determination of Mancunians that Germany was certainly not going to win this war and that that country would eventually pay for what it had done to Manchester and its people.

CHAPTER FOUR

1941

A rather grim new year began with the continuing work of clearing rubble and debris from areas which had been attacked during the Christmas Blitz. Rebuilding would take a long time and, for now, all spare money had to be devoted to the war effort. Nevertheless power supplies, transport and communications were soon restored. Manchester's citizens were devastated by the damage, but were determined. Major air raids were continuing but it was now someone else's turn. The complete destruction which the Germans believed they had wrought on Manchester spared the city from their attentions for a while. In addition, RAF Balloon Command were now in charge of 'Starfish sites' established to try and protect the city. These were decoy targets intended to confuse German bombers into thinking they were bombing the city when in fact they were bombing empty countryside. Each Starfish site (or Special Fire site from which they took their name) had an air-raid shelter for the operational crew and several different devices to simulate lights and fire. The sites were usually built between 4 miles (7km) and 10 miles (17km) from the place they were intended to protect and at least a mile (1.75km) from any village or settlement. Glow boxes simulated city lights. 'Fire baskets' on stands about 20ft (6m) tall contained creosote or coal onto which petrol or diesel was dripped from overhead tanks to simulate exploding incendiary bombs hitting buildings after the attacking planes had passed over. Water was then pumped onto the fires producing clouds of steam which looked like smoke. The 'lights' and 'fires' were controlled from concrete bunkers. It was an extension of a decoy programme designed to protect airfields and factories devised by Colonel John Turner. There were a number of Starfish sites within the area of the south-western Pennines. Nine of those protected Manchester and included two on Chat Moss in Salford and one on Carrington Moss in Trafford. These three sites lie to the west of the city. There were also Starfish sites at Tatton Park, Lyme near Disley

(Lyme Hall was featured as Mr Darcy's house in the BBC adaptation of *Pride and Prejudice*) and at Sponds Hill, close to nearby Kettleshulme; plus one on agricultural land in Reddish on the outskirts of Stockport. These four sites lay to the south of the city and the remaining two lay to the east. There was one on Ludworth Moor/Chunal Moor (two moors which are adjacent to each other) close to Glossop; and one close to Buckton Castle on the outskirts of Carrbrook in Mossley near Stalybridge.

These sites were mainly active from 1941 to 1943 and initially enjoyed some success in diverting German bombs from their real targets, but eventually the Luftwaffe recognized the decoy sites for what they were. Today aerial photography of most of the sites shows no trace of the Starfish decoy features but the concrete control bunker at Carrbrook has survived. Buckton Castle is the desolate, windswept remains of a medieval castle, built on wild moorland, which looks down on the village of Carrbrook, and which, in contemporary terms, requires at least 'moderate fitness' to access. To one side of the feature is a large quarry and the old Starfish bunker lies on the quarry floor close to the entrance, now a part of a more modern building. The quarry is on private land, and there are a number of health and safety issues, so there is no public access. However, the locations of the Starfish decoys demonstrate the complete isolation, on lonely expanses of often inhospitable countryside, necessary for such sites. There were other Starfish sites protecting Lancashire

Looking down on village of Carrbrook from Buckton Castle Starfish site. Manchester can be seen in the distance top right.

All that remains of the Starfish bunker at the Buckton Castle site.

towns to the north of Manchester which also offered the city a little protection. It is a testament to those who operated these sites that they proved so successful under very difficult conditions.

In early March, the Germans carried out more raids, in an attempt to destroy the industrial complex of Trafford. Hulme, one of the suburbs close to Trafford, took another hit which destroyed a row of houses, killing six people, and the Old Trafford football stadium was completely destroyed by a bomb intended for the aircraft manufactories at Trafford Park. In the eyes of Mancunians one of the most significant outcomes of this was that Manchester United had to play at Manchester City's stadium in Maine Road for the rest of the war. Buckingham Palace was also bombed in the same month, prompting Queen Elizabeth (who later became the Queen Mother) to say that finally she could look the East End in the face. Three months later, on Whit Sunday, 1 June, three hours of German bombing damaged Manchester police station and hit the hospital in Salford (Manchester's twin city) killing fourteen nurses, but there was no return to the prolonged ferocity of the bombing that the city had endured during the Blitz.

Winston Churchill on Oxford Road in Manchester, 26 April 1941.
(*Courtesy of Manchester Central Library Local Studies*)

In May there was more curiosity than fear when Hitler's deputy, Rudolf Hess, flew to Scotland on a supposedly secret mission to initiate peace talks between Germany and England. He ran out of fuel and parachuted from his plane, landing just south of Glasgow, where he was handed over to the local Home Guard to be taken to Renfrewshire for interrogation before being imprisoned at Maryhill Barracks in Glasgow. There was much speculation but the true story of his intentions has never been unravelled, or at least never made public. Hess, dismissed by Hitler as a madman, would be tried after the war and sentenced to life imprisonment in Spandau. After Dunkirk in 1940 Hitler had drawn up plans for a military invasion of Britain codenamed Operation Sealion. It never took place but it was in response to this threat that the Home Guard had been established and armed, plus signposts had been blacked out so that any Germans who had attempted a landing would not know where they were or which way they should go and they would also face armed resistance from the Home Guard. By summer 1941 the Home Guard numbered nearly 2 million men and were doing sterling work. Units travelled on bicycles, motorbikes, horses or sometimes in private vehicles. They manned pillboxes (concrete structures built for coastal watching), set up road blocks, placed barbed wire on the beaches, and trained themselves in the use of improvised weapons and explosive devices. Folk were forbidden to gossip and told to always put their country before themselves. There were frequent reminders on posters and in the newspapers that gossip cost lives. Invasion committees were set up in cities, towns and villages to co-operate with the military should the invasion happen. War planning books were kept for use of resources and distribution of food, sanitation and medications; for lists of vehicles, animals and tools; for emergencies and makeshift mortuaries.

People tried to keep their spirits up but 1941 was rather a grim year on the Home Front. Food rationing was in full force and there were inevitable food queues. Imports of alcohol ceased in October and reduced supplies of sugar and barley meant that there were shortages of beer and whisky. There was also a shortage of petrol. The Limitation of Supplies (Cloth and Apparel) Order was passed and civilian clothing was rationed, for the first time, at the beginning of June. Purchases of all types of clothing for everyone were subject to ration coupons in the same way as food. It was hard to keep up with fashions or growing children. The Board of Trade sponsored several

Food queues in Manchester, 1941. (*Courtesy of Manchester Central Library Local Studies*)

ranges of 'utility clothing' which had strict specifications on the amounts of material to be used and the labour involved. No turn-ups were allowed on trousers, nor were double-breasted suits allowed. Skirt and coat lengths were regulated. All utility clothing carried a label stating 'CC41'. This stood for Controlled Commodity and 41 referred to the year this measure had been instigated. Leading fashion designers, such as Norman Hartnell and Hardy Amies, were commissioned to design clothing for the utility ranges and maximum prices chargeable for both cloth and clothing were laid down. Women became adept at making-do and mending by using old clothes and curtains to make new items of wear or by adorning faded clothes with bits of lace or ribbon. Some items, such as silk or nylon stockings, were difficult, if not impossible, to obtain. Many girls and women either wore ankle socks or nothing with their shoes. The armed forces and school uniforms relied on thick lisle stockings which were simply for regulation purposes, and, in winter, warmth, but they were not popular. Most nylon stockings still had vertical seams along their backs and those wanting to dress up and look chic emulated these

Shop rationing and shortages in Manchester, 1941.
(*Courtesy of Manchester Central Library Local Studies*)

stocking seams by drawing them down their legs with charcoal or eyeliner pencils. Lines of 'national footwear' were also produced although the height of heels was strictly limited.

There were lighter moments, however. Radio, cinema and dances were the main forms of entertainment and Mancunians looked forward to their Saturday-night dances or a visit to the cinema. The film of Margaret Mitchell's classic story of the American Civil War, *Gone with the Wind*, made in 1939 and starring Clark Gable and Vivien Leigh, was one of the most popular of the Second World War. Radio, however, was generally the chief form of entertainment and news. The BBC had just two programmes: the Home Service (today's equivalent is Radio 4) and the Forces Programme. The BBC news was the main means of communication of events for many people. Much of it was war news of air raids, land and sea battles, plus the general progress of the war, although there was some home front news as well. Singer Vera Lynn, known as the 'Forces' Sweetheart', was one of the most popular entertainers. By 1945 there were 10 million radio licences held in Britain. Wartime radios were quite cumbersome in comparison to modern sets. The sets were worked by valves and enclosed in polished wooden cases. The speaker was covered in a kind of hessian. There were usually just two knobs on the front: one for volume and on/off, the other to search for radio stations. British Summer Time (BST), the daylight hours saving scheme adopted in 1916, had continued but at the end of 1940 the clocks had not been put back an hour to Greenwich Mean Time (GMT), as was the custom, but had remained on BST. In the spring of this year the clocks were put forward by another hour so that the country was now two hours ahead of GMT. This was dubbed British Double Summer Time (BDST) which remained in force until autumn 1945. In the winter clocks were put back an hour to BST but did not return to GMT until after the war.

One of the most significant and important developments of the entire war took place in 1941 but it would be over thirty years before any information about it was released. Alan Turing, a gifted young mathematician, had pioneered the breaking of the Enigma code at Bletchley Park which was the top-secret government codebreaking and cryptanalysis headquarters. During the 1930s the Germans had developed Enigma machines for encoding radio messages, and distributed them to their armed forces. Shortly before the outbreak of war, the Polish Cypher Bureau, at the Warsaw Conference in July 1939, gave British and French intelligence officers the basic details of the construction and working of German Enigma machines as well as their methods of decryption. The Polish method, however, did not cope well with the Germans changing procedures or details. Turing took a more general approach based on decryption for breaking the codes. Working in the famous Hut 8 he developed indicator procedures which could break the codes used by the German army. The naval Enigma codes had much more complicated indicator systems that were difficult to decipher. Turing worked on this alone at first and eventually solved problems by use of 'sequential analysis' in the summer of 1941. His work was said to have shortened the war by two years, although no-one knew it at the time. Codebreaking and cryptanalysis are detailed and complex procedures and there are several good publications available on the subject as well as information on the internet. Alan Turing's connection with Manchester came in the immediate aftermath of the war. The Victoria University of Manchester appointed him as Reader in the mathematics department in 1948 and the following year he became the deputy director of the computing machine laboratory. Turing worked on programming software for the Manchester Mark 1, the prototype of modern computers, and on artificial intelligence. He developed the 'Turing Test' whose premise was that a computer could be said to think if a human interrogator could not differentiate, through conversation, whether they were talking to a man or a machine. Alan Turing died prematurely in 1954; supposedly committing suicide after being prosecuted and punished for having a homosexual relationship which, at that time, was illegal. His contributions to the fields of crypto-analysis, computing science and mathematics were immeasurably important and unique. Manchester has commemorated him in numerous ways. One of the most poignant memorials stands in Sackville Park, between Whitworth Street and Canal Street. Beneath his statue, which is sitting on a bench, a plaque at his feet reads:

Alan Mathison Turing
1912–1954
Father of Computer Science
Mathematician, Logician
Wartime Codebreaker
Victim of Prejudice

together with a quotation from philosopher, Bertrand Russell, part of which read that: 'Mathematics, rightly viewed, possesses not only truth, but supreme beauty ...'.

The losses at sea sustained by the Axis Powers in the Mediterranean were severe that autumn, with nearly a million tons being sunk. By contrast in November British losses at sea had fallen from 500,000 tons to 180,000 tons per month. This meant that the threat of starvation through the loss of imported food supplies had receded. Although Alan Turing had cracked the naval Enigma codes it was vital that the Germans did not realize this fact and so some naval losses were regarded as inevitable. It was one of the unpalatable facts of war.

Since the outbreak of the war there had been, to some extent, forced choices between meat and munitions imports. It was hoped that this could now be relaxed somewhat. The grain harvest had not been as good as had been hoped during the summers of 1940 and

An armoured car and tanks in Albert Square (Tanks Campaign), Manchester, 18 August 1941. (*Courtesy of Manchester Central Library Local Studies*)

1941 despite the land under cultivation having been increased by 45 per cent. Nevertheless, it was 50 per cent up on 1939 and there were good crops of potatoes, sugar beet, root vegetables and fodder. Dairy cows and cattle for meat were being maintained but poultry was still being neglected despite the promotional efforts made in the Great War and the acute shortage of fresh eggs. Austerity was still essential and Manchester once again suffered more than rural areas where extra fresh food could often be obtained more easily. On the plus side stocks of coal had increased and were now 2 million or 3 million tons larger than the previous year although domestic stocks would continue to be rationed.

A week before Christmas the British government passed the National Service (No. 2) Act. All men and women aged 18 to 60 were now liable for national service which included military service for those under the age of 51. It was the first time women had been conscripted and also the first military registration of those aged 18.5 years old. It also raised the question of conscientious objectors once more. The legislation had made provision for folk to object to fighting on moral grounds. In the first call-up batch of men aged

20 to 23 it was estimated that about 22 per 1,000 registered as conscientious objectors, although by the time of Dunkirk this had dropped
to 6 per 1,000. There were nearly four times as many conscientious
objectors as during the Great War; and there was a register of conscientious objectors containing around 6,000 names of which a third
were women. The question of conscientious objectors was a difficult
one. During the war there were three main grounds: religious, moral
and political. Most objectors fell into the first two categories. There
was a three-tier system for objectors. They could be registered un-
conditionally, registered as willing to do civilian work essential to the
war effort, or registered to carry out non-combatant duties in the
army. The reaction to conscientious objectors was roughly the same
as in the Great War, George Orwell calling them 'ignorant fascists'.
Many still labelled them as cowards. Employers refused to give them
jobs, or, if they did, it was on a very temporary and 'last one in, first
one out' basis. A number of conscientious objectors also had socialist
views which led large numbers of people to condemn all socialists
as conscientious objectors. They came from all walks of life and all
strata of society. Many of the conscientious objectors simply said that
they could not take human life but they were willing to work in non-
combatant roles. This was accepted and many of them were sent to
the front where they worked as medical orderlies, drivers, auxiliaries,
dispatch riders, mechanics and clerks, or did essential war work such
as mining, agriculture, forestry or in hospitals. The main problems
were caused by those who refused to contribute in any way. Fenner
Brockway, from Stockport (now part of Greater Manchester), and a
leading conscientious objector during the Great War, said during the
Second World War that '. . . the conscientious objector has no right to
reject war in the present unless he spends his life in helping to make a
future without war . . .'. Local military tribunals were set up, as they
had been during the Great War, before which conscientious objectors
pleaded their case. The views and principles of tribunal officers
towards conscientious objectors were all important and rejections of
objectors' claims varied between 6 per cent and 41 per cent. The arguments before and against remained the same as during the Great
War. On the one hand people felt that they had the right to choose
whether to fight or not and the freedom to follow their conscience. On
the other hand, especially with an adversary like Hitler, it was
absolutely necessary for others to fight, and perhaps to die, in order
for them to have that freedom of choice. 'Some wars just have to be

fought' said one sadly, and a tribunal chairman, on hearing a pacifist's objection to fighting, turned and said 'Even God is not a pacifist for He kills us all in the end'. One Mancunian conscientious objector won his plea not to be sent to fight at the tribunal hearing of his case, but he was willing to contribute to the war effort generally and he was sent to work in the mines. He remained working as a miner until after the war was over when injury finally forced his retirement from the job. Another Manchester pacifist refused to pay the fine imposed on him for not enlisting and was sent to Strangeways for twenty-eight days. The cells were freezing and there was a rule of total silence. He spent his days in a workshop and was then locked up in his cell from 4.00pm in the afternoon until the 6.00am the following morning. If the air-raid sirens went off the prisoners remained locked in and the lights went off. The officers then went to their air-raid shelter, leaving the prisoners in total darkness and silence to pray that the bombs wouldn't hit the prison.

As well as military conscription there was also what was termed 'industrial conscription'. From May 1940 the Minister of Labour and National Service had the authority to '... direct any person to perform such services which in the opinion of the Minister the person directed is capable of performing ...'. This was so that essential industries, such as food provision, armaments, munitions, shipbuilding and aircraft manufacture, for example, would not suffer from labour shortages and be unable to fulfil their obligations. Tribunals had scant patience with objectors to industrial conscription and there were several imprisonments. Included in the industrial conscription was compulsory firewatching duties. Some conscientious objectors maintained that, although they would always help fellow beings in distress, they would not register for any job that was part of the war effort. This kind of objection was usually summarily dismissed and those objecting were either fined or imprisoned. Many organizations and individuals refused to employ conscientious objectors and their families were given a hard time. Wives would be ostracized and their children taunted and bullied. Memories were long and even after the war was over conscientious objectors continued to suffer. After the Great War they had been banned from voting for a period of five years. This time there was no such authoritarian redress but social shunning played a great part. The Peace Pledge Union and the Quakers supported conscientious objectors throughout the war but there was little they could do about post-war social exclusion and it was often the children of conscientious objectors who suffered most. A rare story of a conscientious objector which brought smiles to the faces of many Mancunians appeared in the *Manchester Guardian* during the winter of 1940. A conscientious objector, working as a quarry labourer, appealed to the tribunal to have his name struck off the list of conscientious objectors and to be issued a military certificate so that he could serve in the army. In his letter he wrote that

> ... you must not regard the statement I made as false, but I want you to understand that my wife has been doing nothing but nagging since I received my conscientious objector's certificate ... please make it possible for me to hear no more about this objector's business and arrange for me to be medically examined and called to the colours with men of the 20–22 class in my area ... I am awfully sorry to cause this unnecessary trouble but I would rather be in the armed forces for the rest of my life than stay at home with my wife for another month.

Much to everyone's amusement the tribunal granted his request, but history is silent on what became of either him or his nagging wife. In the spring of this same year, the *Guardian* reported on another conscientious objector from Lancashire, who worked as a riveter. He had told the Manchester tribunal that because he was black he had struggled to get a job and now he had it he did not wish to give it up. He did not wish to do military service anyway because he had tried to join up before the war but he had been rejected simply because he was black. The tribunal chairman asked him if it would alter his opinion if he were to be treated as an equal. The black guy shook his head sadly. 'There is no freedom for the coloured man', he said. 'We do not get treated as equals'. The tribunal chairman sympathized with him in being a victim of prejudice, and complemented him for being frank and honest, but nevertheless it was insisted upon that he do military service. The whole question of conscientious objectors was a thorny one and the debate still continues today.

The Schedule of Reserved Occupations was also abandoned and occupations for females on the Home Front were now restricted by the requirements of the war. Those leaving school had three choices. They could work in the factories, much of which involved war work and making ammunition, they could work on the land as a member of the Women's Land Army, or they could train as a teacher. Many young women found these options disappointing but accepted that they had no choice. This writer's mother chose teaching so that she would have a profession she could follow after the war had ended, reasoning that work in the factories and on farms might be limited when the war was over and the men returned home. Teaching young children had long been seen as 'women's work' and, while she chaffed at that description, the idea of helping to guide the young minds of the future generation appealed to her. Anyone who told her she was just doing that job because she would get long holidays soon realized that they had made a serious error of judgement.

The Land Army, or the Land Girls as they were known, worked long, hard hours for low wages in often poor conditions but most of them enjoyed the work and the camaraderie. Their uniform consisted of a green jumper, brown trousers, brown felt hats and a khaki over-coat, and their badge depicted a wheatsheaf which was symbolic of the work they did. Tasks included milking cows, lambing, looking after poultry, ploughing, harvesting, digging ditches, muck-spreading, cutting out foot-rot in sheep and applying Stockholm tar afterwards, or doing any other work required about the farm. A separate timber corps, known as the 'lumber-jills', cut down trees, managed wood-lands and operated sawmills. Those who worked in factories often worked on munitions and armaments, but they could find themselves doing a wide variety of jobs. One girl began by making haversacks for military personnel before being deployed to making light suits for soldiers, and then working in an aircraft factory helping to manu-facture turrets for Lancaster bombers. Women also largely staffed the munitions factories, cotton mills, hat-works and catering establish-ments. Factory hours were long and finding the time to queue when shopping for various foodstuffs became extremely difficult. Although women were conscripted for work in factories from 1942 onwards, many men were free with their complaints. Dinner would not be on the table when they returned home. The home was not as they would like it. Their children were being fed from tins and not being looked after or disciplined properly. Even worse, some women earned more than their husbands and, in the men's eyes, this was shameful indeed. The resulting exhaustion and stress suffered by many women was hardly noticed. Munitions work could be difficult and dangerous. The girls who worked in the munitions factories were known as the 'canary girls', exactly as they had been in the Great War, because constant contact with the chemicals involved turned their skin yellow. While some women's hair might turn blonde because of the exposure to chemicals, natural blondes sometimes found their hair turning green. Although the work was comparatively well paid there was little training given and few safety measures. When an accident did occur it was often horrific. The *Daily Telegraph* reported on an accident which happened in a Lancashire ordnance factory as trays of anti-tank mine fuses were being filled. One of the fuzes exploded and set off the rest of them in the tray.

> The girl working on that tray was killed outright and her body disintegrated; two girls standing behind her were partly shielded from the blast by her body, but both were seriously injured, one fatally. The factory was badly damaged: the roof was blown off, electric fittings were dangling precariously; and one of the walls was swaying in the breeze ...

There was (and still is) a belief that the only real work is paid work. This ignores the fact that much, if not most, of the work done in Britain during the war was unpaid and done mainly by women. Women fulfilled roles of housewives, mothers, volunteers, helpers etc. They were responsible for cooking, cleaning, washing, making or mending clothes for their families, bringing up the children, volunteering to help with the war effort, helping in air raids or with evacuations, providing treats for the troops ... the list was endless and all the jobs were unpaid. If a woman had children under 14 (school leaving age) at home she was not required to work outside the home at a paid 'day job'. However, the contributions made by these women were not only valuable but essential to the smooth running and mobilization of the country and its fighting forces. Even if they did do any paid or voluntary work, their domestic responsibilities remained central to their lives. Many women in Manchester took paid work as a necessity rather than a choice, whatever their status. They might take in washing or offer dressmaking and childcare, jobs which could be done in the home, to earn a little extra to meet the ever-rising costs of living. Those who couldn't frequently felt guilty. Britain was the most fully-mobilized country in the Second World War. A third of the population was engaged in war work and aircraft production trebled. However, although women filled jobs in industry, services and business, much as they had done during the Great War, they still had to contend with low wages, long hours and opposition from men. Much to the horror of many men, especially pilots, the Air Transport Auxiliary (ATA) allowed women to serve as pilots. They did not go into combat but flew planes which were used as trainers and transports and they also delivered bombers to airbases by flying them there. The first eight female pilots recruited flew only Tiger Moths, but, as recruitment numbers and skills increased, women were eventually allowed to fly most aircraft. In July 1941 Hurricanes were flown by women and in August that same year Spitfires were flown by female pilots. A total of 166 female pilots flew during the war, eventually succeeding in gaining the respect of their male colleagues and receiving equal pay for the work.

Manchester had a thriving aircraft industry throughout the war. A.V. Roe, whose aircraft manufacturing company was known as Avro, was founded by Alliott Verdon Roe in 1910 at the Brownsfield Mill on Great Ancoats Street. Subsequently manufacturing and development sites at Alexandra and Woodford (Stockport) were established. Avro developed the Avro 679 Manchester at the beginning of the war but the plane was underpowered. It was the forerunner of the much more successful four-engined Avro Lancaster.

Avro had an experimental station at Ringway Airport on the edge of the city (known today as Manchester Airport) where the planes were tested. The original Rolls-Royce engines were replaced by Vultures in 1940 and the use of Bristol Hercules engines was also considered. Other aircraft manufacturers connected with Manchester included Metropolitan-Vickers at Trafford (who also produced electrical equipment for the Beyer Peacock railway workshops in Gorton,

The Avro Manchester bomber. A 'Real Photograph' taken in 1942.

an outer suburb of Manchester) and Fairey Aviation at Stockport (both now part of Greater Manchester). The Manchester was designed with a twin tail and rudders, both used in the later design of the Lancaster derived from it. Avro built a total of 177 Manchesters and Metropolitan-Vickers (bombed in 1940 and 1941) built thirty-two of the same aircraft while Fairey Aviation built numerous models of the Handley Page Halifax plane. The re-designed Manchesters were flown by 207 Squadron of Bomber Command and RAF Coastal Command. Early in 1941 the first model of the Lancaster appeared, sporting four Rolls-Royce Merlin engines and longer wings. Subsequently the original Manchesters were used for training from 1943 while the Lancaster remained in service until the end of the war. More than 7,000 Lancasters were manufactured, around 3,000 of them in the Manchester Avro factory at Stockport (now part of Greater Manchester) and a number of Manchester girls and women were employed to build the constituent parts.

As well as fully-paid occupations, the roles of official voluntary organizations were also incredibly important. The two main ones were the Air Raid Precautions (ARP) and the Women's Voluntary Service (WVS). The ARP, which had both male and female members, organized public air-raid shelters and ensured that blackout regulations were kept. Windows had to be either painted black or to be heavily curtained with very dark material. The ARP also helped in the aftermath of air raids, searching for survivors and providing first aid to casualties. The WVS had a uniform of a green felt hat with a red band, grey/green coat, dress and skirt and a red blouse. It was a completely voluntary organization. They assisted with the evacuation of schoolchildren all over the country, made bandages, knitted or sewed clothing and comforts for the troops, and ran canteens at ports and railway stations for members of the forces. Jobs could range from the cleaning of children's gas masks to collecting salvage to cooking meals and arranging housing for those who lost their homes in air raids. The WVS has sometimes been referred to as 'the army that Hitler forgot'.

December was, overall, perhaps the most notable month. In the first week the Japanese bombed the US fleet at Pearl Harbor in Hawaii, and an indignant United States finally entered the war. Japan had been fighting in the Far East for some time. China had become a unified country during the 1920s but the increasingly militaristic Japanese had felt that they should be the ones to rule Asia and began with an invasion of Manchuria. Although this was repelled they succeeded in capturing Beijing in 1937. Despite General Chiang Kai-shek's best efforts, the Japanese also captured Shanghai and Nanking. Consequently, when the European war broke out, China sided with the Allies while Japan sided with Germany and Italy (the Axis powers). Now that America had become involved, it led to hundreds of thousands of US servicemen being sent to Britain. There was little rationing in the States and the US military brought nylons, chocolates, perfume and cigarettes with them, all of which were in extremely short supply in Britain. They also brought with them the brand-new dance craze of the jitterbug and the music of Glenn Miller. All this delighted British girls and women, if not the British men who saw the Americans as rivals, and it gave rise to the popular male lament that the Yanks were 'over-paid, over-sexed and over here'. It didn't help that many Mancunian families hosted US servicemen during the Christmas periods throughout the course of the war. The American servicemen were far from their own families and friends and appreciated the friendliness and generosity of their hosts; an appreciation they showed by gifts of food, alcohol, cigarettes and nylons. Folk had been discouraged from sending many Christmas cards so that the postal deliveries would not be clogged up, leaving the way clear for more important mail. There was pressure to spend money on war bonds rather than presents, so children's gifts were usually homemade, but the talents and ingenuity of parents were amazing. They made doll's houses, toy carts, stuffed animals, sweets, dolls, and even gas masks for dolls, sewed or knitted garments for children and their toys. Traditional foods suffered from rationing but, as in the Great War, many cooks managed to find acceptable alternatives. More wealthy folk, profiteers or black-marketeers as they were called during the war, could usually obtain goods that were either rationed or virtually unobtainable. The black market was, however, condemned as 'treason of the very worst kind' and, in the House of Commons, punishments suggested for black marketeers included long prison terms, heavy fines, and one MP called for whipping with a 'cat-o-nine-tails', a whip made from 'nine knotted thongs of cotton cord' designed to cause maximum pain and laceration of the skin. This did not happen but it demonstrated the anger and resentment felt by so many at the selfishness and greed of profiteers and their customers. On Christmas Eve this year Winston Churchill dined at the White House with the American President,

Franklin D. Roosevelt, and it was pointed out that the menu especially reflected the wartime sacrifices being made in the United States, but to Mancunians it was hardly a menu of wartime economy. The meal consisted of several courses and luxury foods including: oysters on the half shell with crackers; clear soup with sherry; celery and assorted olives; thin toast; roast turkey with chestnut dressing, sausage, giblet gravy, beans, cauliflower, casserole of sweet potatoes, cranberry jelly, and rolls; grapefruit salad and cheese crescents; plum pudding and hard sauce; ice cream and cake; coffee, salted nuts and assorted bonbons. In contrast, British newspapers were advising folk to eat 'mock roast chicken' (a leg of lamb) or a 'mock chicken loaf' (made from rabbit or veal) followed by caramel fluff or cherry topsy-turvy pudding for their Christmas meal. Turkey was unaffordable for many in Britain and chicken was a luxury during the war and remained so until the 1970s. Mancunian families scrimped and saved their ham and bacon rations and anything else which might help to make something of a special festive meal. Most items were rationed and the 'icing' on the Christmas cake was made from wartime marzipan paste which consisted of mashed potato mixed with a tiny bit of sugar and egg white together with a few drops of vanilla essence, and then browned in the oven. There was no icing as such because of sugar rationing. Other Christmas treats for those on the Home Front included toasted date sandwiches, date pudding, or dried fruit and potato tart, a pastry case filled with a mix of mashed potato, raisins, dried egg, a little almond essence and a bit of honey. Just before Christmas a further system of rationing was introduced. This was a points system aimed mainly at tinned and processed foods which were in increasingly short supply; especially as such foods were needed for military forces serving overseas. Tinned meat, fish and fruit were included in the points system along with condensed milk, rice and breakfast cereal. Each person had 16 points per month, controlled by points coupons issued in the ration books with other coupons for rationed fresh foods, although goods in the points system could be purchased anywhere, not just from the customer's locally-designated shop for rations. The allocation was not overly generous. All the points could be used buying a single can of meat or fish, or 2lbs (just over 900g) of dried fruit, or 8lbs (3.6kg) of split peas. At the same time whale meat and canned fish from South Africa were available and not rationed, but they did not prove popular with

British consumers who have always tended to prefer their own traditional foods. American Spam, a compressed bacon-based luncheon
meat, was only just acceptable. It was a difficult time but hunger and
adaptation played a large part in the creativity of cooks who all tried
to make the best of the reduced and rationed food situation. In any
case, in Manchester, this year, memories of last year's Christmas Blitz
had driven almost everything else from most peoples' minds and
Christmas 1941 was a generally low-key affair in the city.

CHAPTER FIVE

1942

The Manchester Stock Exchange began 1942 with quotations resuming upward trends which made for better business activities. Home railway stocks seemed to be giving some cause for concern but the textile trade was quite buoyant, with both Lancashire Cotton Corporation and Fine Spinners' shares rising. The chemical industries, like Imperial Chemicals and Courtaulds, were also doing well. Iron and steel industries were a more mixed bag with heavy electrical engineering and machine tool foundries doing well but interest in pig iron had declined. The steel trade was healthy but its structural material supplies were moving slowly. Overall, it was not a gloomy forecast. The Refuge Assurance Company, based on Oxford Street in Manchester, was doing well for itself with health insurance, life insurance and death insurance policies, and also reported a significant increase in the 20–29 age group of people taking out insurance policies. The company invested in war loans and by the end of 1941 had £6,249,300 (£251,200,000 today) in government war loans.

Warship Weeks (ships for the Navy), Weapons Weeks (tanks and guns for the Army) and Wings for Victory Weeks (to help the RAF by purchasing bombers and fighter planes) were held regularly in towns and cities around the country. At the end of February in 1942 the Manchester National Savings Committee, based in Mount Street, held a Warship Week with the aim of raising enough money to adopt a battleship, HMS *Nelson*. Some 200 volunteers were asked to make model battleships for promotional displays in local shop windows. Blueprints and instructions were supplied by the National Committee in London for volunteers to use in making the models from wood or cardboard. The city had a number of large investors who donated to this scheme as well as middle income and small savers. By the end of the week an amazing total of £12,524,967-1s.-8d (£503,400,000 today) had been raised. This was substantially more than the target of £10,000,000 (£401,900,000) which had been set and Manchester could

A Bren gun carrier leading an artillery battery during Manchester Warship Week,
27 February 1942. (*Courtesy of Manchester Central Library Local Studies*)

feel justifiably proud of itself. After the success of Warship Week,
HMS *Nelson* was adopted by Manchester and served with honours in
the Mediterranean, Sicily, Salerno in 1943, and Normandy in 1944.

Although the city was not a rural area itself, Manchester took a
keen interest in rural affairs since they directly impacted on the
well-being of its citizens. Farming was having its usual tough time
and the Ministry of Agriculture felt that the harvest of 1942 could
well be critical for the country. Farmers were also being asked to give
detailed crop plans for 1943. One of the problems was that 80 per cent
of farms were no larger than 150 acres and small farmers were
making little more than farm labourers. Adequate drainage was also
a problem as a good deal of land was badly drained. There were a
number of drainage schemes and the Ministry was hoping to have up
to 400 excavators to loan out for this purpose by the end of the year.
There were also 7,000 tractors available for hire to farmers. Once
again there was a threatened shortage of agricultural labourers as
male workers were conscripted but the Women's Land Army was
working hard to make up the shortfall. There was concern, however,

that some farms were being compelled to grow crops for which they were either ecologically or economically unsuited. However, 6 million more acres had been ploughed than in 1941. There was already over a million acres of potatoes and there would be 4 million tons of vegetables produced this year. In addition, there were 4 million acres of oats and nearly 500,000 acres of sugar beet. Lack of feed was affecting some pastoral farmers. Dairy farming remained constant but sheep and poultry farming had declined. During the Great War fresh eggs had been more freely available and in the Eastern Counties there had been concerted efforts to expand and promote the poultry industry. Although meeting with some success, keeping hens continued to remain more of a cottage industry with the result that when war came there was an acute shortage of eggs once again. During the Great War four fresh eggs per week per adult had been the allowance. Now it was just a single fresh egg per week. The absence of fresh eggs was partly compensated by the use of powdered egg. One of the most frequent complaints about food during the war was about powdered egg. The dried egg powder was imported from America and one tin was the equivalent of a dozen fresh eggs. It was used in cake mixes or recipes where the taste was disguised but its use for scrambled eggs, omelettes or in egg-based sandwich spreads was often disliked. The single fresh egg a week which was allowed was much treasured by folk. Government's attempts to extoll the virtues of powdered egg fell on deaf ears and a number of people simply preferred to go without. It was worse for towns, as Manchester discovered, because keeping hens in urban areas was difficult due to many people having no gardens.

A month after the outbreak of the war, the Ministry of Agriculture had coined the slogan 'Dig for Victory', the inspiration for which they had borrowed from the Great War when David Lloyd George had urged the population towards self-sufficiency. This was followed up by a poster advertising campaign, jingoism in the forms of song and poetry, and a number of booklets advising on what to grow, when to grow it, and how to grow fruit and vegetables efficiently. Part of one song, aimed at older children, ran

Dig! Dig! Dig! …
And keep on digging
Till we give our foes a wiggin'
Dig! Dig! Dig! To Victory!

At the same time a Ministry booklet carried a picture of a 2- or 3-year-old child on the front, dragging a small spade and hoe with him and carried the message that no one was too young to help. This was another lesson which had been learned in the Great War. The often quoted ideal was a lady in Dorset, who, with only the help of her two young sons, had produced: 60 bundles of asparagus; 50 bundles of rhubarb; 80lbs of tomatoes (36.2kg); 600 lettuces; 10 bushels of spinach (363.6kg); 20 bushels of onions (727.3kg); 2 hundredweight of carrots; 2 hundredweight of parsnips; 3 bushels of artichokes (109.1kg); 120lbs (54.4kg) of peas; 210 pounds (95.2kg) of runner beans; 2 sacks of broad beans; 10 bushels of beetroot (363.6kg); 210 vegetable marrows; 30 cucumbers; 3.5 tons of potatoes. (NB 2.2lbs = 1kg. 1 bushel = 36.4 kg)

Again, as in the Great War, gardens, flowerbeds, parkland and public land were either given over or commandeered for the growing of vegetables. Orchards supplied apples, pears and plums while gooseberries, red and black currants, were harvested from bushes in cottage gardens. Blackberries and raspberries grew wild and were often picked by children. In Manchester, where gardens were at a premium, the city's parks and public land were given over to growing vegetables. Piccadilly Gardens in the city centre were divided into allotments and carefully tended by citizens. Nationally there were nearly 2 million allotments and over 3 million private gardens. It was calculated that these could produce vegetables worth £10,000,000 (£402,000,000 today) to £15,000,000 (£603,000,000 today) each year. Vegetables were divided into three rough categories. Group A, root crops, included potatoes, carrots and parsnips. Group B, winter greens, included cabbage, kale and sprouts. Group C, termed miscellaneous, included peas, beans, onions and tomatoes. The general aim was to ensure a year-round supply of fresh vegetables. Certain fresh foods were actively promoted. A home-made drink called Carrolade, made from the juices of carrots and swedes, was advocated, as well as curried carrots and carrot jam. Potato skins were deemed the most nutritious part of the plant and folk were encouraged to eat them, whether baked or boiled. Lord Woolton, Minister of Food 1940–3, had the job of promoting the benefits of rationing to the public. One result of this was his favourite 'Woolton Pie'. This consisted of 1lb (0.45kg) each of diced carrots, potatoes, swedes and cauliflower, three/four bunches of spring onions, one teaspoon of vegetable extract and one teaspoon of oatmeal. These were cooked together in water for ten minutes, drained, put in a pie dish and covered with a crust of wholemeal pastry. It was then oven-baked until the pastry was cooked and served hot with gravy. Unfortunately, this pie was not the success that Lord Woolton had hoped for but there were a number of mainly vegetarian recipes around during the war owing to the scant rations of meat, eggs and cheese. Spam, a word whose meaning has changed entirely in the twenty-first century, was a compressed bacon-based luncheon meat imported from America and sold in small loaf-shaped tins. It could be eaten hot or cold. Despite the derision Spam drew, both during the war and afterwards as the ultimate in poor man's cost-cutting, it is, in fact, quite tasty and a very palatable alternative to bacon or chops. Vegetarians surrendered their meat coupons in return for extra cheese rations. Diabetics surrendered their sugar coupons and were given extra meat rations and sometimes extra butter as well. Those serving in the armed forces or doing heavy jobs such as mining, agricultural or forestry work, were given extra rations of meat and cheese. Lessons had been learned from the Great War that rationing, fair shares for everyone and plenty of fresh food would ensure a healthier population which would be needed for efficient resistance if Germany did invade Britain. Pig clubs were also set up. Pigs were bought from money collected through locally-organized schemes and fattened on scraps. Then the animals were slaughtered and shared out between members of the club. Pig clubs in the centre of Manchester were simply not feasible but in some outer suburbs, like Gorton, Northenden or the Ivygreen allotments in Chorlton-cum-Hardy, there was a chance they could flourish. Keeping hens was also encouraged but again this was only viable in the outer suburbs of the city or where someone had a really large garden. Manchester was at a disadvantage to its country cousins for there was always more food available in rural areas. The British Restaurants were doing well providing meals across the country and many were making a profit. There were limitations in that no meal could be more than three courses and there was an upper cost limit so that more wealthy folk could not hog food. Most meals were a cheap set price. As in the Great War this was of benefit to the general health of people, especially poorer folk, and infant mortality fell to 49 per 1,000, an all-time low. There was still much general discontent, however, about the 'national loaf' which was like wholemeal bread and mostly regarded as 'grey and mushy', but at least it wasn't rationed. Many Manchester working folk had become used to poor or restricted diets and, for some of them, food rationing was particularly beneficial in that they were no longer excluded from obtaining fresh produce, meat and cheese, whereas before they had been simply by the high prices engineered either by hoarding or by profiteers. In June the Combined Food Board was established to co-ordinate food

St Augustine's RC Church, York Street Chorlton-on-Medlock, Manchester 1942. (*Courtesy of Manchester Central Library Local Studies*)

supplies from around the world to the Allies, with particular attention paid to supplies from Canada and the US. By August most
foods, apart from bread and vegetables, were rationed. Fish wasn't
rationed but, although prices were controlled from 1941, it became
very expensive because the trawlermen constantly ran the risk of
attack from German U-boats. Fruit supplies were limited. Lemons
and bananas became unobtainable, giving rise to the song 'Oh yes,
we have no bananas ...'. Oranges were in short supply and mainly
reserved for children and pregnant women. Apples in the shops were
usually limited to one per customer. Ration books were like gold dust
because, without them, folk could not obtain food supplies. Despite
the rationing and the hardships, the general health of the nation was
declared to be good. As in the Great War, everyone getting some
share of everything had been very beneficial.

There was some severe rationing of other commodities as well.
Clothing coupon points were reduced from 66 to 48 per year and the
number of buttons, pockets and pleats allowed on clothing items was
restricted. Soap was also rationed to 4 coupons per month. A single
coupon would buy either one small bar of soap or a small packet of
soap flakes. There was a shortage of paper and supplies were limited,
with newspapers reducing publication to 25 per cent of their pre-war
levels. The publishing industry suffered and titles went out of print.
Wrapping paper was prohibited. Central heating was not allowed
in the summer months and domestic coal was rationed to 2,200lbs
(1,000kg) per year. At the beginning of July the civilian petrol ration
was abolished which meant that fuel was no longer available for
private car owners. In this case Manchester was not hit as hard as its
country cousins because its citizens still had the use, albeit limited, of
trams and trains. Gas-bag vehicles were also used. This involved a
large bag of 'street or town gas' being carried on its roof to power a
vehicle. Manchester Corporation had a number of gas-bag buses in
use during the war.

There was also a severe shortage of timber available for manufacturing furniture. Demand for new furniture had been heavy in the
wake of the bombings. Consequently, a Utility Furniture Advisory
Committee was established in 1941 and it was decided to ration new
furniture to newly-weds and those who had lost their homes through
bombing. The Domestic Furniture (Control of Manufacture and
Supply) Order became operative in November 1942. There were a
number of approved furniture designs and a catalogue was published

Manchester Corporation gas-fuelled bus, 1942.
(*Courtesy of Manchester Central Library Local Studies*)

early in 1943. Designs were simple and unadorned in the style of the Arts and Crafts Movement. Items were basic and functional. The same logo, 'CC41', was used for utility furniture as had been used for utility clothing, and the two commodities became known colloquially as 'the two cheeses'.

The April 1942 Budget was not welcomed but was regarded as inevitable. There was a whole raft of tax changes which mostly favoured those on low incomes. This was beneficial to the lower-paid, although the government secretly hoped that the extra cash these low-paid workers saved would somehow find its way into the war effort. However, purchase tax doubled, from 33.3 per cent to 66.6 per cent and the tax on entertainments was also increased. Whisky prices went up by 25 per cent. Beer, tobacco and cigarettes rose in price. The price of clothing had also risen but the government decided to take strict control over clothing price increases and also to ensure the promotion of utility clothing ranges. The introduction of tax reserve certificates for companies and corporate bodies, which encouraged advance provision for taxation, proved popular and £200,000,000 (£8,039,000,000 today) of certificates had already been issued. Land tax was reduced to the pre-war rate as the owners of undamaged properties were being forced to pay more land tax than the owners whose properties had suffered war damage. A tax allowance of £10 (£402) for additional travelling expenses was extended to all employed folk. There was also discussion of post-war reorganization.

Crime and its increase proved a serious and time-consuming worry during the war. Theft and looting were the most frequently-committed crimes. Looting became so serious at one point that it carried the death penalty but this was never carried out, the punishment usually being a heavy fine and/or imprisonment. Thefts were also frequent and those from allotments were among the most despised. Others tried to charge folk for allotted spaces in public air-raid shelters. Sexual assaults on women increased during the black-out which was an unpleasant side effect of using complete darkness to deter the German bombers. Then there were the hoarders and profiteers ('spivs' as they were commonly known) who made money out of black-market goods, such as cigarettes, alcohol, certain luxury items and foodstuffs, which were normally very scarce. Ration-book fraud could cause problems and so did those who broke the government's wartime regulations as a simple protest against all the restrictions. Manchester gained notoriety with its own infamous forger, Herbert Winstanley, who lived in Rusholme, a suburb close to the city centre. He hid a complete forger's workshop at his home and throughout the war he forged thousands of pound notes which he kept hidden, stacked in neat bundles. He was only caught in 1945 when he placed a bet in Salford using forged notes and received a ten-year sentence for his crimes. He was known locally as the 'King of Forgers'.

It was in the summer of 1942 that El Alamein, a small Egyptian town and railway halt on the Mediterranean coast, entered the general consciousness of the British public. The first battle of El Alamein (1–27 July) was fought in Egypt between the Afrika Korps of the Axis forces commanded by Field Marshal Rommel (the Desert Fox) and the British Eighth Army commanded by General Auchinleck. The Axis forces were coming dangerously close to the cities and ports of Egypt, although the Allies had so far managed to prevent further advances. The Second Battle of El Alamein (23 October–11 November) was then fought with Lieutenant General Bernard Montgomery

(Monty as he became affectionately known) replacing Auchinleck as commander of the British and Commonwealth forces. The resulting victory for the Allies ended the Axis threat to Egypt and the Suez Canal as well as to the Persian and Middle Eastern oilfields, and marked a turning point in the North Africa campaign.

Although the Manchester Regiment, which served in Europe, India, Singapore and the Far East during the war, was not directly involved at El Alamein, Manchester citizens were still absolutely delighted at the victory and joined enthusiastically with the rest of the country in ringing church bells on 15 November (for the first time since May 1940) to celebrate the Allied victory at El Alamein. The euphoria would not last but its timing, shortly before Christmas, gave morale a much-needed boost. Coincidentally, on the day that the first Battle of El Alamein had ended indecisively, Manchester suffered another air raid, although this time by just a single aircraft. The bombs hit the inner suburb of Beswick at breakfast-time. They killed three people and injured seven seriously, caused numerous lesser injuries and damaged three streets of houses.

The government remained keenly aware of the fact that British society was far from equal. There had been no 'land fit for heroes' after the Great War, only another two decades of austerity, and this was causing severe problems for millions of people who had already

The Manchester Regiment marching to Albert Square in Manchester in 1940.
(*Courtesy of Manchester Central Library Local Studies*)

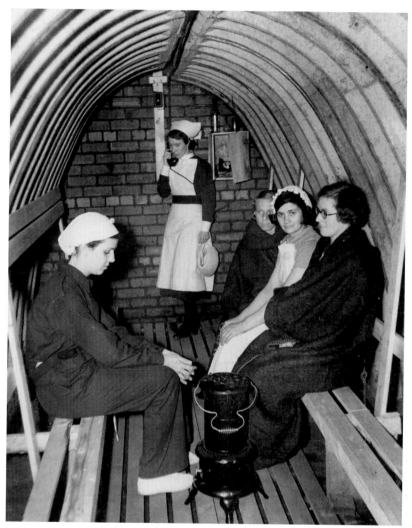

Subterranean air-raid shelter, Manchester 1940.
(Courtesy of Manchester Central Library Local Studies)

given all of what little they had. In an attempt to address the problems and to keep low-income workers and the poorer sections of society on side, Sir William Beveridge had been commissioned to write a report proposing the beginnings of a social security system. The report, over 300 pages long, was published on 1 December and its basis was to 'introduce a system of social insurance from cradle to grave'. Beveridge believed that all workers should pay a weekly contribution which would then be paid back in benefits to cover sickness, unemployment, retirement or being widowed. The main points of his report were:

- Proposals for the future should not be limited by 'sectional interests' in learning from experience and that a 'revolutionary moment in the world's history is a time for revolutions, not for patching'.
- Social insurance was only one part of a 'comprehensive policy of social progress'. The five giants on the road to reconstruction were Want, Disease, Ignorance, Squalor and Idleness.
- Policies of social security 'must be achieved by co-operation between the State and the individual', with the state securing the service and contributions. The state 'should not stifle incentive, opportunity, responsibility; in establishing a national minimum, it should leave room and encouragement for voluntary action by each individual to provide more than that minimum for himself and his family'.

There was already free hospital treatment available for war casualties but the groundwork for the introduction of a National Health Service had been laid and Beveridge argued, against much opposition, that the recommendations in his report would also provide a minimum standard of living. What was really needed to guarantee this was a minimum wage, which was the dream of workers, trades unionists and strikers alike in the Second World War. However, many in the middle and upper classes felt that this might encourage fecklessness and idleness among the working classes. Seventy years on there is a minimum wage but the jury is still out on whether this is a necessity, and out of this has been born the idea of zero-hours contracts, something that neither Beveridge nor the wartime workers would ever have countenanced. The *Manchester Guardian* called the report 'a big and fine thing', while the *Daily Telegraph* said that it was 'a consummation of the revolution begun by David Lloyd George in 1911'. The Archbishop of Canterbury declared that it was 'the first time anyone had set out to embody the whole body of the Christian spirit in an Act of Parliament'. It was a revolutionary concept which represented the beginnings of a more enlightened and compassionate attitude towards social welfare. Since the beginning of the Industrial Revolution and before, it had been the practice, especially among the upper classes, to lay the blame for poverty and unemployment on the poor themselves. The idea of a fair day's pay for a fair day's work was seen as a rather startling new concept, since in Victorian England the aim had generally been to keep wages as low as possible on the grounds of efficiency and economy. It was felt that the need to work for long hours just to earn enough money for food and shelter would inspire folk to work hard rather than having to increase the costs of production by paying higher wages and thus encourage the idleness which might result from shorter hours. Low wages and rising prices meant in many cases that workers 'had to run just to stand still'. It was time for change. Although Churchill was lukewarm about the whole thing (he would subsequently vote against the foundation of a National Health Service) he and the government agreed in principle but stated that folk would have to wait until the end of the war before the recommendations could be implemented. It was frustrating but people generally accepted that they would have to wait awhile for the concessions they had won. Churchill was a Conservative prime minister leading the nation in wartime, not a Labour leader for social issues in peacetime.

For the first time since the Blitz of Christmas 1940 Manchester folk felt they had something to celebrate, although food, clothes and fuel were more strictly rationed than ever and there were few toys in the

Tank in action in the Second World War. Manchester raised funds for tanks as part of the war effort.

shops. War savings, discouraging 'frivolous spending' and encouraging investment in the British war effort, were being heavily promoted by the National Savings Committee. Folk were encouraged to make their own toys and gifts. The children of Manchester in the Second World War had very different expectations for Christmas presents and most were delighted to receive a single toy, an orange and perhaps a few sweets. Christmas decorations were also home-made, the most popular being paper chains made from interlocking strips of brightly-coloured paper glued together. Small Christmas trees, about 3ft (1m) tall were also in demand so that they could be taken into air-raid shelters. The Battle of El Alamein might not have brought families' loved-ones home to them but it had been a victory that would, everyone believed, bring the end of the war a little closer.

CHAPTER SIX

1943

In early April the government published a white paper by the economist John Maynard Keynes proposing a plan for post-war currency stabilization which would create an international banking system. Of far more interest to Manchester's citizens, however, was the April Budget of £5.8 billion of which 56 per cent was to be raised from current revenue. The remaining deficit would be £2.8 billion of which £2.2 billion would be borrowed at home. Although most Mancunians were not trained economists, they got the clear message that the war required extensive funding and that they, along with every other ordinary citizen in the country, would be paying for it. Most were not averse to tightening their belts and making fresh economies if it would help to defeat Germany but there were also fears and grumbles about the rising costs of living, the falling values of wages, the large profits being made by some companies, and the fact that the better-off did not seem to be paying their fair share. Churchill had attempted to outlaw strikes at the beginning of the war but, backed by their trades unions, workers insisted on fair pay and fair treatment. In 1941 Lancashire engineering apprentices had gone on strike, initiating the first serious wartime industrial dispute. This was followed in 1942 by strikes at the Royal Ordnance Factory in Nottingham and in the Tyneside shipbuilding yards. In September 1943 workers and apprentices at Vickers Armstrong of Barrow, who manufactured ships, tanks and armaments, walked out on strike over poor pay and bad conditions.

At the end of July in 1943 Ernest Bevin, the Minister for Labour and National Service, had announced that women aged between 19 and 50 would be called up to work in aircraft and munitions factories and that men eligible for military service could opt to work in coal mines. Since September 1939 experienced miners had been enlisting in the armed forces causing labour shortages, as had happened during the Great War, while other miners had been able to

find better-paid jobs in essential war work (reserved occupations).
It was hoped that the mining labour shortages would be filled by the
unemployed but this did not happen. By the middle of 1943 the
mining industry was in desperate need of 40,000 miners. Coal production slumped and by December Britain had just three weeks' supply
of coal in reserve. Voluntary requests for new miners had made little
impact so Bevin introduced a scheme whereby a proportion of conscripted men would work in the mines instead of being drafted into
the armed forces. This was done by means of a ballot. As a result,
48,000 'Bevin Boys' were sent to work down the mines. Half had
been selected by ballot, which denied any choice of serving in the
armed forces. The other half were volunteers who preferred mining to
the armed forces. The ballot was simple. Every month a number was
drawn from a hat. All men whose National Service Registration
Number ended with the same number were sent down the mines.
Refusal to accept could mean a fine or imprisonment. The 'Bevin
Boys' were sent to work in the various coal mines of England, Wales
and Scotland, and represented about 10 per cent of those aged 18 to
25 called up during the last two years of the war. There was a great
deal of resentment among those chosen, and especially for those
young lads who had dreamed of honour in the armed services it was a
bitter disappointment. There was also the added frustration of mis-
understanding by the public. Mining was a vital necessity to the war
but many saw it as a way of dodging combatant service, although it
could be as equally dangerous as fighting at the front. Mining conscripts came from all classes and all regions. There were a number of
government training centres, mostly in England, where they received
a basic six weeks of training before being sent down the mines.
Conscripts usually lived in Nissen huts adjacent to the mines where
they worked. The initial experience of descending hundreds of feet
below ground to work in the cramped, silent, airless, twilight must
have been terrifying, especially for those who suffered from claustro-
phobia. Most worked with the pit ponies or on the conveyor belts
alongside more experienced men but some worked at the coal face
itself. The National Coal Mining Museum near Wakefield has pre-
served a coal mine which the public can visit to experience how
miners lived and worked. It is a terrifying learning curve which
renders the word 'respect' quite inadequate. About twenty people are
crammed into a wire cage measuring little more than 6ft (180cm) ×
4ft (120cm) which descends jerkily 550ft (around 170m) down into

the earth. There is no electric light. Each person is given a miner's lamp which is the only illumination. Cameras, phones and watches have to be left at the surface. It is dark, dirty, dank, damp and smells incredibly musty. Water drips down the walls of the shaft. Once in the mine there are lots of long narrow passages in which it is impossible for people over 5ft (150cm) tall to stand upright. At the coal face miners often had to sit or crouch to work the coal from the rock. Battered wooden doors were kept closed between each section to minimize the spread of any fire. The rock presses in on all sides. Air quality sometimes fluctuates which can leave folk hot and breathless with a pounding heart. Pneumoconiosis (known as 'black lung' by miners) is a dust-based lung disease, which was a fatal occupational hazard for miners. In the Second World War there were few mechanical aids and it is an understatement to say that the work was hard, dangerous, and unrelenting, for both men and animals. There were very few female miners. Apart from the nature of the job, females, although they may have greater stamina, don't usually have the same physical strength as men to deal with large or heavy objects. When pit ponies were used, they spent most of their time underground with just a few rest days, particularly Bank Holidays, above ground. In the mine, small stalls were cut into the rock for them to be tethered when resting. There was a stone trough at one end and just sufficient room for the horse not to have to stand upright all the time. Many of them also died below ground. The Lancashire coalfield was one of the biggest in England and there were collieries in Manchester's outer north-eastern suburbs of Bradford, Clayton, Moston and Newton Heath, as well as a number in the area of what is now Greater Manchester. However, questions concerning age, experience and wages loomed large and there were 'pit-boys' strikes in 1942 and 1943 involving young miners who were angry at earning less than their older colleagues. Matters would come to a head in 1944.

In the House of Commons Dr Edith Summerskill led a call for equal pay for women. She stated that in the auxiliary services women were replacing men 'head for head' but, although men were asking and obtaining the going rate for the jobs, women were paid well below that rate, at only two-thirds that which the men received. Yet members of the ATS worked as dispatch riders, electricians, motor mechanics and cyclists; those in the WRNS did clerical work, were radio operators and transport drivers; and women in the WAAF worked as wireless mechanics, electricians, aircraft hands and

ATS members near Manchester, c.1941.

armourers' assistants. In addition, it was suggested that there should be a special wartime domestic corps for women with its own uniform. Dr Summerskill also said arguments put to her that women would deprive men of jobs in a competitive labour market were rubbish. Surely, she said, it was efficiency, not sex, which should be the benchmark. The calling up of women in the 45–50 age group was criticised as well, when it was felt that there were younger women who could be called upon, but the government had in mind nursing, midwifery and hospital services which required older women with more experience. This raised further protests that jobs seen as 'women's work' were traditionally low paid which was why there was now a shortage of midwives, nurses and servants. Manchester, most of whose women already worked extremely hard for lower pay than men, followed this debate with great interest. Taxation, as ever, was a sore point, and even worse was the question of wives' post-war credits. During the Budget debate in April the government admitted that 'working wives had posed a problem tax-wise' and that the Treasury had tried to solve the problem by 'treating a wife as a mere appendage of her husband and sent post-war credits to the husband alone'. They had done 'a thoroughly illegitimate thing. Tax was deducted at source and at the end of the war it was proposed to hand over to the husband that which the wife had paid. At the least the wife should be informed that she was entitled to a post-war credit and be able to ascertain the precise amount from the revenue authorities.' Manchester women were appalled. It was as though time had slipped backwards over half a century and more. Their mothers and grandmothers had fought long and hard for the recognition that women were people too, who should have their own rights, and that they were not just the invisible servants and playthings of men to be treated as their whims dictated. Lady Astor supportively joined in the debate by quoting the numbers of women variously employed. She said that there were 17.5 million women aged between 14 and 65; 10 million of these women were married, looking after homes and caring for 9 million children; 7 million women were employed in the military services and industry; and 2.5 million married women were employed. The response she received was simply that the figures might not be accurate and that it might also be inadvisable to publish them on security grounds, but the reasons why this might be so were never given. However, a number of MPs insisted that the government had a duty to revise pay and working conditions for women and that there should be equal pay for equal jobs; and, furthermore, that public opinion supported this view.

The bombing capacity of the Lancasters led to them being chosen for the famous Dam Busters raid on the Ruhr in May 1943 by 617 Squadron under Wing Commander Guy Gibson. It was known as Operation Chastise. A special 'bouncing bomb', developed by Barnes Wallis, enabled a drum-shaped bomb to bounce at high speed across the surface of the water and avoid the heavy torpedo net barriers intended to protect the dams. The Ruhr and Eder valleys were specifically targeted because they were heavily industrialized as well as providing hydro-electric power, pure water for making steel, drinking water and water for the canal transport system. The Möhne and Edersee dams were bombed and partially destroyed, flooding the Ruhr Valley and the villages of the Eder Valley. A third dam, the Sorpe Dam, only sustained minor damage. Two hydroelectric power stations were destroyed and several others damaged. Mines and factories in the area suffered a similar fate and 1,600 civilians, including Russian prisoners of war, were drowned. It was a severe blow to the

Germans. Eight of the nineteen Lancasters sent on the mission were shot down and fifty-three aircrew were killed but, despite the sacrifices, it was hailed as a great British success.

However, there was a growing concern about German reprisal raids 'any night anywhere' as revenge for Allied raids and bombing attacks on Germany. In Manchester there were regular firewatching rostas administered by the AFS. Ellen Wilkinson, a Mancunian who had risen to be Parliamentary Secretary to the Ministry of Home Security, felt that fire was the greatest danger from these raids and that the numbers of firewatchers needed to be increased. The government was accused of indecision, delay and vacillation, as well as too much official red tape, in the way that the firewatching (or fire guard) service was administered, which caused much friction and resentment. There was also the question of payments to firewatchers. It was stated that about 100,000 firewatchers were paid around 2 shillings (£3.84) an hour for doing what nearly 5,000,000 other folk did for nothing. The money was coming out of the public purse and not out of the individual employers' pockets. There was a plan to provide comprehensive fire cover, working with the National Fire Service who would provide more powerful equipment for the firewatchers. Both males and females were working efficiently together to provide an effective civil defence. It was felt that the country was divided into front and backline areas, with the coastal regions of the east and south forming the front line and the rest of the country forming the back line; and most agreed that this was a fair assessment. The experience of the Blitz, however, was still raw and uppermost in most Mancunians' minds. There were claims of a matter of injustice which had been created in Manchester in respect of wartime fire prevention. In the Trafford Park area there were 150 companies where the Ministry of Aircraft Production had become the fire-prevention authority and a levy had been placed on these firms for this purpose. However, it was claimed that manufacturing businesses on one side of the Ship Canal had to pay the levy whilst those on the other side did not.

In September Benito Mussolini was stripped of power by the Italian king, Victor Emmanuel III, and arrested. The southern part of the country signed a peace treaty with the Allies while the northern half remained firmly in German hands. Germany was outraged at the Italians' defection from the Axis. Louis de Bernières' story of Cephallonia, a Greek island immortalized in *Captain Corelli's*

Mandolin, was one result of Mussolini's overthrow which definitively demonstrates German attitudes and reactions to Italy switching sides. The Italian commander on Cephallonia had decided to try and resist German attempts to disarm his forces. After a ten day battle the Italians suffered 1,300 casualties and several thousand more Italians were taken prisoner and massacred in one of the worst German war crimes. Mancunians did not know what to make of the Italian situation. There was still much distrust and dislike of their former friends and many Italian men remained interned on the Isle of Man, in Scotland or abroad.

During the war Britain managed to entirely mobilize its population, both male and female. Like the Great War twenty years before, it was seen as a 'people's war that enlarged domestic aspirations and produced promises of a post-war welfare state'. In the Great War, women had kept the home fires burning and carried out the men's jobs while they were away as well as supplying the soldiers and sailors with 'comforts' (clothes, food, tobacco, books etc) and in doing so had gained the vote for themselves, much more independence and the promise of 'a land fit for heroes' to which their husbands could return. The 'land fit for heroes' did not materialize but now folk believed that their efforts in this war would earn them a welfare state with adequate housing, education, social benefits and healthcare for all. This was why Britain had been so successful in mobilizing its home front and much of this success was again due to the mobilization of its women. The women supported the war effort, ensured that the rationing of food and clothing was successful, ran the communal British Restaurants, carried on the 'make do and mend' tradition and spearheaded conservation drives for paper, metal and bones. Paper was not the only commodity collected on a regular basis. Re-cycled iron was of great importance to the steel industry and scrap iron was needed for the manufacture of armaments such as tanks and Spitfires. Whitworth Street Park and Phillips Park, like a number of other Manchester parks, lost their iron railings for the war effort. Women also offered their services to the military; worked in the factories producing munitions, Spitfires, Hurricanes and Lancasters; and served in the Women's Land Army and the WVS. Voluntary services had become important, providing lunches for schools and hospitals, overseeing evacuation and billeting of children, and organizing all manner of things from raising funds for the war effort to caring for old folk and children. By April 1944 Didsbury had collected £120,204 (£4,376,000 today) towards its £500,000 (£18,200,000) target. The pressure for war savings was kept up and there was a 'Wings for Victory' display in Piccadilly which featured a bomber pitted with shrapnel scars. Manchester women had long known about cooking tasty dishes from scraps of food; making do and mending; conserving everything that they could; working hard in the factories or on a voluntary basis; and they made a huge contribution to the mobilization effort. On a more individual note, one Manchester lady further camouflaged her family's Anderson shelter by planting daffodils in the earth covering its roof. The children helped as well. A school in Hulme collected war savings stamps at 15/- each (£28.80 today), converted them all into war savings certificates, and managed a grand total of £300 (£11,520) for the Michaelmas term of 1943. Another boy raffled an onion for £1.00 (£38.41). A young Chorlton-cum-Hardy lad, who had climbed onto the roof of his house so he could better see the fires caused by falling bombs in Manchester, noticed two people with flashlights on the adjoining roof. Knowing that only small torches with Number 8 batteries were allowed at night for walking the streets, he climbed back down and ran to tell his father. An ARP warden was alerted and the couple with flashlights were arrested. It turned out that they were trying to provide guidance for Luftwaffe pilots on their way to bomb Liverpool. This action was deemed to be treason and they were imprisoned in Strangeways to await the death penalty. It was a sombre end to a year in which ever-increasing restrictions, rationing, rules and regulations were conspiring to make daily life very spartan for most folk.

CHAPTER SEVEN

1944

The question of food supplies was still high on the agenda. It was reported that food stocks were adequate and the only shortage might be milk. Efforts were still being made to ensure regular supplies at a price acceptable to everyone. Milk was rationed, as in the Great War, but the weekly allowance had been reduced from 4 pints (just under 2 litres) to 3 pints (1.5 litres). It was considered vital that growing children should have milk, because it provided calcium for their growing bones and teeth; but it was also required for sick people and nursing mothers. However, it was hoped to increase the cheese ration from 2oz (60+g) to 3oz (90+g). The quality of strawberry and raspberry jam needed to be improved and apricot pulp had been bought in from Spain to make apricot jam. The 'wonders of dehydration' were discussed by Parliament. What this basically meant was the drying of vegetables which could be re-constituted as needed but would take up much less storage and carriage. The Minister of Food quoted the case of 1,000 tons of cabbage dried and reduced to 40 tons. He then went on to enthusiastically describe a new product: '... mashed potato powder, which was contained in a tin much like cocoa powder ... one took a few teaspoons, poured hot water on it and got a very good mashed potato without any cooking in the home ... I do not think anyone would know that it was not ordinary mashed potato'. To the generation which grew up on 'Smash' this statement might raise a few smiles. It is an interesting experiment to prepare mashed potato from both the dried powder and the natural way by boiling and mashing potatoes and then assessing the taste of each. The main problem with dried foods is that in many cases some of the nutritional value is lost in the process. Provision of food supplies to the military services was essential, of course, but the Minister of Food would not reduce the food stocks at home to the detriment of the nation's health. Rationed provisions could not face further cuts. Trade agreements were still in place with Australia and New Zealand for beef, mutton, lamb and dairy products; and with Canada for bacon and cheese. Jamaica, South Africa and Southern Rhodesia were being encouraged to continue the concentrated orange juice scheme. There was a glut of herrings and salt herring curers were being encouraged to cure and kipper larger quantities of herrings than usual which the government would undertake to purchase. Mancunians welcomed fresh foods but were much more reserved about dried vegetables from tins. There was still a large Irish population in the city and one of their staple dishes was colcannon, a mixture of fresh cabbage and potato, with sometimes onions and bacon added. They were not about to sprinkle powder into a dish and reconstitute it with hot water. It would not have the same bite at all. The Minister was not really listening. He was concerned that there might be a world food shortage and wanted more than just a four-year plan for agriculture. Salads were expensive and he thought that most people could do with a little more protein in their diet. The 'seas were teeming with fish, and if one thousandth part of the time was put into fish production that was put into agricultural production, the food shortage would largely disappear ...'. However, trawlers with crews were necessary to catch fish and he wanted the Admiralty to release some of the trawlers they had commandeered so that large-scale fishing could be resumed.

The question of post-war tax credits for wives had only partially been resolved. The Chancellor said that the certificate was usually issued to the husband when some other tax related form or notice was being sent to him. Notice of assessment in respect of a wife's earnings was not sent to her but to her husband. There were murmurings of discontent and it was hastily added '... under a new arrangement which is now being introduced ... at the same time as the notice is sent to the husband the wife will be sent a separate notification, either at her home address, if known, or at her place of employment, notifying her that the certificate for the previous year is being issued ...'. This would explain her rights and stated that where husband and wife agreed apportionment the credit would be divided accordingly. This arrangement would only apply to wives who were in employment and paying tax which was deducted from their wages. However, it could not be guaranteed that the notification to the wife would be sent at the same time as the certificate went to the husband. It was a far from ideal arrangement. All that could be said was that it was an improvement of sorts, but Mancunian women were not generally impressed and many felt that their husbands still controlled their earnings.

Mining conscripts continued to be resented by the long-serving miners who feared they might take their jobs after the war and in 1944 miners went on strike for an increase in wages. They also resented the fact that munitions workers, often females, earned more than they did and had better opportunities for overtime. It was a little ironic in view of Dame Edith Summerskill's recent call for equal pay for women. However, the miners, along with thousands of other working-class men, felt that women should be in the home, not out earning a wage, and that, as soon as the war was over, this is what should happen. The strikes were spearheaded by the Welsh miners. The average wage for a miner was £5 per day (£182 today) but the average industrial wage had now reached £6.10s.0d (£236.60), a fact that brought the Manchester, Lancashire and most other miners out on strike. D-Day was looming and the strike attracted a great deal of criticism in the British and the American Press. The *Chicago Tribune* reported the bare facts but said that the strikes and the 'slow-down' policy adopted by the miners had earned them general condemnation. 1944 marked the peak of all wartime industrial action, with over 2,000 stoppages and the loss of nearly 4,000,000 days' production, to the point where even the Trades Union Congress (TUC) felt duty-bound to support a wartime defence regulation that outlawed any incitement to strike. The *Daily Mail* furiously condemned all the strikers as unpatriotic communists and those serving abroad felt, as soldiers and sailors had done in the Great War, that strikes at home in wartime were a kind of treachery. However, as one miner commented '... the argument that a strike would let our soldiers down was countered by men who had brothers and sons in the forces who, so they claimed, had urged them to fight and maintain their customs or privileges. They argued that they must retain something for those absent ones to come back to, while the suggestion that we should wait for further negotiations was swamped by the reply that we had already waited a long while ...' Mancunians, who had already lived for 150 years with low pay, poor conditions, and high mortality, while mill owners got rich quick, had some sympathy. Manchester workers understood the needs of war but felt that if a company was making decent profits then some of it should be ploughed back into the business to make their lives a little easier, which would in turn enhance company profits further through more efficient and effective contributions from its workers. They were acutely aware that 'the land fit for heroes' promised after the Great War had not materialized and probably never would. Instead they had suffered from continued austerity, the General Strike, hunger marches, the Wall Street crash and the Great Depression in the twenty years between the wars. Now they were being asked to give everything once again to another war. The National Arbitration Tribunal, however, was unsympathetic to the miners and sided with the employers, so, in the end, the government was forced to intervene, much to the annoyance of Churchill who had tried to outlaw strikes at the beginning of the war. Differentials had to be restored and in the end the miners obtained one of the highest minimum wages in the country. There might have been more vociferous protests if a new threat from the Germans to British towns and cities had not emerged.

The summer of 1944 had brought a fresh menace from the skies. This was the V-1 flying bomb, the 'buzz bomb' or 'doodlebug' as it was nicknamed because of the buzzing sound that was one of its chief characteristics. It was a monoplane which had no pilot. The fuselage was manufactured from welded sheet steel and the wings were made of plywood; and its 'Argus-built pulse-jet engine pulsed 50 times per second' which is what produced the dreaded buzzing sound. The V-1s were either ground-launched, using a rocket-powered catapult, or air-launched from a bomber. They were unable to take off independently due to the low engine thrust and problems with the small wings. Code-named 'Cherry Stone', the V stood for Vengeance weapon (*Vergeltungswaffen*) but it initially had a limited range (150 miles/ 240km) and most were fired at London or Southern England. The missile was pre-set to trigger the arming of its warhead after about 37 miles (60km) and when the detonating bolts were fired the V-I went into a steep dive which caused the engine to stop. The sudden silence alerted those below that impact was imminent. Mancunians were both fascinated and terrified although the south-east was bearing the brunt of the attacks. The first attack took place on London in June 1944. The British response was immediate and quite successful. Barrage balloons, anti-aircraft guns and fighter aircraft brought down about 80 per cent of these little menaces. A few of the missiles failed to explode which made a dangerous and difficult task for bomb-disposal officers. Sinister as the doodlebugs had been, the V-2 rocket was an even more terrifying 'vengeance weapon'. It was a long-range ballistic missile and it was manufactured to attack Allied towns and cities in retaliation for the Allied bombings of German cities. These missiles travelled faster than the speed of sound and rose as high as 50 miles (81km) above the ground when fired, sometimes destroying themselves on re-entry into the atmosphere. Their 1,000kg warheads could create a crater 66ft (20m) wide and 26ft (8m) deep. The first V-2 attack was in September 1944. The speed and trajectories of these missiles made it impossible for them to be intercepted by fighters or anti-aircraft guns, and there was no guidance system which could be jammed. Both V-1s and V-2s were expensive to manufacture and so slave labour from the concentration camps was used in the rocket programme to keep down costs. Like the rest of the country, Mancunians were seriously frightened, but although the V-2s had a greater range and accuracy than the V-1s, the main attacks were made on London, Ipswich and Norwich. However, the Luftwaffe were also using Heinkel He 111 bombers to cross the North Sea and launch V-1s, so that they now had a greater range. Between 100 and 150 flying bombs were being fired each day. Doodlebugs hit their targets about half an hour after launching. Mancunians, remembering the Christmas Blitz of 1940 and dreading a renewal, were not particularly reassured that they would be spared from fresh attacks, despite the emphasis on the south and east of the country. They were right to be concerned. Early in the morning of Christmas Eve 1944, almost four years to the day after the Christmas Blitz of 1940, the Germans launched a total of forty-five V-1s against Manchester but fourteen crashed in the North Sea so that only thirty-one made it across the Channel into Yorkshire. Of these, just seven reached the area known as Greater Manchester and the one which fell at Didsbury was the single successful hit in the city and suburbs of Manchester, detonating in a field of sprouts close to the River Mersey. There were no deaths or injuries but there was some damage done to property in Didsbury, Burnage and Northenden. Hitting a field of sprouts was probably not regarded by the Luftwaffe as their finest hour. The remaining six fell on towns like Stockport and Radcliffe, but the one which caused the most damage missed its intended target, landing instead on Tottington, a small Lancashire town between Bury and Ramsbottom (both now part of Greater Manchester). The bomb hit a row of cottages, killing seven and injuring thirteen, and left a crater 30ft (9m) deep. The remaining twenty-four flying bombs intended for the city landed in the surrounding counties of Cheshire, Derbyshire and Yorkshire. The bomb which hit Stockport fell on

Garners Lane. Two houses were destroyed, several others damaged, and a car was burned out, but amazingly only one person was killed, although there were some seriously injured. Around 150 American soldiers helped with clearing the damage and securing homes. In the Manchester area the damage and destruction caused was comparatively minor, certainly far less than the Germans had hoped. In total 42 people were killed and 109 were injured, 51 of them seriously. Although those numbers were bad enough, they were not on the scale of the Blitz four years before. Buildings up to a mile from the impact sites were damaged, but there was no widespread destruction. Once again, the Germans had missed the aircraft and munitions factories, as well as the railway marshalling yards and lines of communication which they had hoped to destroy. While Mancunians' nerves were badly frayed, it was felt by some that they had a guardian angel who had decided that the city had suffered enough from the Blitz of Christmas 1940. Desperate efforts were now being made by military staff and engineers charged with the task of Operation Crossbow, which was to develop some sort of defence against the larger and more deadly V-2s, but it seemed hopeless. The problem was only really resolved when Montgomery (Monty) finally captured the launching areas in 1945.

However, despite the flying bombs, the RAF had already established air supremacy. As one government minister put it, 'had not the Luftwaffe been outfought in the air, hammered on its airfields, and smashed in its factories, there could have been no invasion of Normandy ...'. The proposed invasion of Normandy (code-named Operation Neptune and the largest invasion by sea in history) had begun on 6 June. It was the prelude to Operation Overlord which would begin the liberation of German-occupied territories in north-west Europe. Amazingly, this highlighted a problem of the numbers of deserters from British forces which loomed large in the summer of 1944. Between that date and 31 March 1945, there were almost 36,400 cases of desertion. Without ration books or identity cards deserters often turned to crime or looting in order to survive. Although in Germany the penalty for desertion was death, this did not generally happen in England. Sentences of penal servitude or hard labour were usually handed out instead. Nevertheless, in Britain, desertions increased, perhaps encouraged by memories of Dunkirk. Although the D-Day campaign took longer than had been expected, the operation was a victory for the Allies and the beginning of the end for the

Germans. On 12 November, the German battleship *Tirpitz*, the sister-ship of the *Bismarck*, was sunk by British Lancaster bombers equipped with 12,000lb (5,443kg) 'Tallboy' earthquake bombs. Over a thousand German sailors were lost. The 'relentless battering of the German war machine', as the *Manchester Guardian* termed it, had begun. Allied bombing was now on a massive scale. As confidence in eventual victory grew a new 'dim-out' had replaced the 'blackout' in September. This meant that lighting the equivalent of moonlight, was now allowed, although a full blackout would be re-imposed if the alert sounded.

This writer's father took part in the D-Day landings and the fighting at sea afterwards. He was born in Marple (now part of Greater Manchester) and won a scholarship to Manchester Grammar School. After leaving school he trained as a radio operator and joined the Merchant Navy. The British merchant fleet was the largest in the world; essential for the transport of food, fuel, equipment and raw materials, and, in wartime, essential for also carrying troops and military supplies. Although they often had naval escorts, merchant ships were vulnerable to U-boats and mines. The major battle in which the Merchant Navy was involved was the Battle of the Atlantic which the Allies finally won in May 1943. This, however, did not remove the danger of mines and U-boats. This writer's father was a member of the crew of the *Empire Jonathan* and, later, the SS *Denewood*. The prefix 'Empire' meant that a ship was one of a group in the service of the British government for the duration of the Second World War and beyond; while 'SS' simply stood for 'steam ship'. As the war progressed he came to have some empathy for what he termed 'the ordinary German sailors' whom, he felt, were just young men like himself, ordered by their government to fight or face the consequences. While he hated fascism and utterly detested Hitler, the SS and the Nazi High Command, he felt guilty about the deaths of some of these young sailors whom he had to fight during his Merchant Navy service. The guilt stayed with him and he couldn't shake it off, even after the war had ended. He drank to block out unwelcome memories and eventually drank himself to death in his mid-50s, as much a victim of the war as if he had been killed in military service. He was not alone.

The Secretary of State for Education, R.A. Butler, was credited with steering the Education Act 1944 through Parliament. There had long been concern over access to education for children from the working classes and poorer sections of society, particularly in the northern cities, and folk were more aware than ever that a decent education system for every child would be essential for future generations to cope with an increasingly complex and mechanized world. It was also recognized that girls would have to be included in this plan as well. The dismissal of female intelligence, abilities and achievement in previous centuries had to be reversed. Already far too much female potential had been wasted. Old attitudes might die hard but now it was essential that they should be altered. Females had demonstrated in both World Wars that they were just as capable as men of working at different jobs and contributing to society and that they could no longer be relegated to the kitchen or the nursery. This new innovative legislation would provide more time at school and free secondary education for all children without all the hidden costs and inequalities that would affect poorer children. Under the Act, Local Education Authorities (LEAs) were required to submit proposals for the reorganization of secondary education into three main categories, grammar, secondary and technical, as recommended by Sir William Spens' report in 1938. Allocation to a particular category would be by means of an examination taken at eleven years old which would be subsequently known as the 11+ exam. The intention was to provide equal opportunities for all children through a tripartite system of education. There would always be differentials in the potential of children. Some would be more academically inclined while others would be more practically minded. In Manchester this Act was seen as incredibly important to the city's children. For too long many working-class children had been denied the opportunity for education through discrimination and lack of money. Parents who could not afford to let all their children stay at school usually favoured boys over girls because there were far more opportunities available for boys and because of the frequently mistaken notion that most girls' ambitions were simply to marry and have children. The school leaving age was also raised to 15 with a recommendation that it should be further increased to 16 after the war. Juvenile delinquency had remained a problem and the government now required all young people over 16 to register and offered them an increasing number of options including clubs and organizations which they could join and take part in activities. The usual reasons were given for delinquency and included absent fathers, working mothers, lax discipline and watching the wrong kind of films. Young people have rebelled against their elders since time immemorial but in wartime it was an unwanted distraction and the vandalism was just an expensive and unwanted nuisance. It was essential that the enemy was not inadvertently given a helping hand by youths being stupid. By providing a number of alternatives it was hoped that youngsters would be distracted from mischief making. The importance of the young replacement generation had long been recognized and there was great incentive to ensure that they were well-trained and educated to cope with the demands of an increasingly difficult and complex world.

Christmas 1944 was still comparatively austere but it was now generally accepted that the tide of war had turned and that victory would not be long in coming. It gave hope to all those separated from loved ones; especially those for whom the separation could be measured in years.

CHAPTER EIGHT

1945

The Second World War might have been the second 'war to end all wars' but life goes on, according to the familiar cliché, and that was certainly true of business life. Lloyd George had said during the Great War that wars were now fought on profits, not principles, and in this respect little had changed. In January, the government found themselves having to consider the request for a utility order respecting fur items made by the Board of Trade. Furs had been considered a luxury trade but harm was being done to London's reputation as a world centre for fur marketing and processing. It was stated that 'any advantage which the general public may derive by way of cheaper fur coats and jackets is entirely incidental . . .'. In addition, there was a request to limit purchase tax to 16–23 per cent (instead of the standard 66.6 per cent rate) in respect of fur goods. Furriers also wanted specifications as to which linings would be used, either utility or non-utility cloth, but pointed out that supplies of utility linings were 'tight'. However, fur traders lamented that all this was too little and too late. The English market was denuded of skins suitable for the manufacture of low-priced fur garments and besides much business had been irretrievably lost to New York over the previous two years. Most Mancunians, reading this item in the *Manchester Guardian*, raised their eyebrows in disbelief and wondered if those in the luxury fur trade actually appreciated there was a war on and exactly how much effort and sacrifice was being made on the Home Front to ensure victory. In any case their more immediate concern was the state of the cotton industry. There seemed to be a decline in American stock market cotton dealings, and, nearer to home, Platt Brothers in Manchester were unable to publish their long-awaited tome on *Modern Cotton Spinning and Doubling* due to wartime paper restrictions. The utility clothing schemes and the drive to 'make do and mend' for the sake of economy had done little to help the industry and it was hoped that its fortunes would improve once the war was over. On a more positive note, a possible new place for re-establishing one of Lancashire's surplus cotton mills had been reported at Dirre-Daoua in Ethiopia. During the Italian occupation, output had been mostly aimed at the white population and only one mill catered for the Ethiopian population. The mill was currently leased by an Anglo-Egyptian-Ethiopian concern, producing only 500 tons of yarn and grey sheeting each year, but could be expanded to an economic size for the niche market of indigenous Ethiopian custom. The cotton industry knew that it needed bold action and new outlets if it was to survive at all because the industry was now struggling.

The bombing of Dresden by the RAF and the USAAF took place between 13 and 15 February. It was an intense and prolonged attack which, ultimately, was in revenge for the vicious ravages of the Blitz, and a kind of turning point. The RAF sent 722 heavy bombers together with 527 from the USAF and dropped nearly 4,000 tons of high-explosive and incendiary bombs on the city. This created a fire-storm which destroyed the city centre and an estimated 25,000 lives were lost. Mancunians, remembering the inferno of their own city created by the Germans, not to mention the terrible mess made of other cities like London, Liverpool and Coventry in the Blitz, felt the Germans were now getting a long overdue taste of their own medicine, but there were a number of citizens who shuddered at the huge loss of civilian lives, especially those of children. They recalled only too well how it felt to lose their own families. At the same time, they understood that it was the German military machine which had caused their sufferings, not the civilians of German cities, and they sympathized to some extent with how it felt to be bombed without mercy. Two further USAAF raids on Dresden followed which were aimed at destroying the city's railway yards and there was yet another one in April on the neighbouring industrial areas. In the seventy-plus years since the bombing of Dresden claim and counter-claim have been furiously argued. Was it necessary? Was it an over-reaction? Was it just German propaganda which made it seem so bad? Was it an 'innocent city of culture' or a centre of munitions and armament manufacturing? Was it simply an attempt to scare the Germans into surrender? It was all of these things and none of them. To read accounts of the bombing of Dresden is dreadful. To read accounts of the Blitz on British cities is dreadful. To read accounts of atrocities in the concentration camps is dreadful. In war, dreadful things happen, as perfectly illustrated by the Great War, but the arguments and counter-arguments about Dresden, rather than the Blitz, look set to continue for decades, if not for centuries. The real tragedy is that it seems human disputes cannot be resolved by civilised debate or by lateral thinking, but only by the numbers of dead on a battlefield.

Hitler committed suicide on 30 April and the surrender was signed by the Germans a week later. VE Day or Victory in Europe Day was celebrated on 7 May by the Commonwealth countries, 8 May in Britain and Europe and 9 May in the Channel Islands. Manchester was intoxicated with relief and joy. There was dancing in the streets of the city, with scenes of wild rejoicing and triumph at the victorious outcome in Piccadilly and the city centre. Vera Lynn's wartime songs, like 'The White Cliffs of Dover' and 'We'll meet again ...', were sung over and over again. The flags of Allied countries hung from buildings

Children's VE Day party in Rosamund Street, Chorlton-on-Medlock, Manchester, 8 May 1945. (*Courtesy of Manchester Central Library Local Studies*)

and there was a civic procession at the Town Hall. Street tea-parties for children, with cakes and jellies, were held in Burnage, Heaton Park and several other city locations, as well as several impromptu parties for adults. Many commodities were still rationed, and, despite all the celebrations, some pubs were forced to remain closed due to a lack of supplies. Alcohol, though, was not really necessary to fuel the sheer joy and exuberance that Germany was defeated, Hitler was dead, and peace had come again. Lights shone once more in windows everywhere, Victory bonfires blazed, and the church bells rang out. The war was not completely over, however. The Allies were still at war with Japan and Japan was not yet ready to surrender.

Although demobilization of troops would start soon, other wartime conditions would continue, and chief among these was rationing. Rationing would remain for some years and even increased in the case of certain commodities. To the astonishment of Manchester citizens, allowances of meat, bacon, cooking fat and soap were further reduced only two weeks after VE Day. For foods that weren't rationed there was still the points system. Each person had 24 points to last them four weeks. Points were in addition to money paid for the goods but it meant, for example, that no one could buy more than two large bars of toilet soap per month. This was aimed not only at rationing supplies but also to deter hoarding and profiteering. Some foods cost large numbers of points; others were not so bad. A pound (just under 500kg) of rice required 8 points; a tin of baked beans 2 points; a pound of currants needed 16 points while a tin of sardines only took 2. Folk still had to plan carefully and needed to remember their ration books and their points allowances if they were away from home. Everyone was allowed 4 soap coupons for four weeks, a large tablet of toilet soap cost 2 coupons. Clothing coupons were also scarce. Each person was allowed 24 clothing coupons which might have to last up to a year. It was not an overly generous allowance. A man's overcoat required 16 coupons, a suit 26 coupons, a pair of trousers 8 coupons and a pair of underpants 4 coupons. The ladies fared little better. A dress needed 7 coupons, a nightdress 6, a mackintosh 16 and knickers were 3 coupons a pair. Making the coupons last, or affording special clothes like a wedding dress, became a great skill. Make-do and mend was very much the order of the day. Coal, coke and paraffin supplies were also limited. Mancunians were further amazed when, after the war was over, bread was finally rationed.

Victory scene in Manchester on VE Day, 8 May 1945.

(Courtesy of Manchester Central Library Local Studies)

It had not been rationed during the war and folk had raised their hopes of being able to eat white bread once more. They had also hoped that the end of the war would ease the situation for the cotton industry but clothes rationing did not end until March 1949, nearly four years after the war had ended. The hatting industry also suffered in a similar fashion; although that was mostly centred on Stockport and Tameside (both now part of Greater Manchester). Hats did not require any clothing coupons but they were prohibitively expensive resulting in most women wearing a headscarf and many men either going hatless or wearing the northern trademark flat cap. Those citizens of Manchester who had hoped for, or could afford, a holiday after the war had ended, found that the railways were sadly depleted. During the war freight and military requirements had been the primary factors. Rolling stock was ageing and a considerable amount of it had been damaged by enemy action. Train services were curtailed and running times uncertain. The times of austerity were certainly far from over, although on 16 June the Family Allowances Act was passed awarding mothers a tax-free cash payment for each child. It was the first time in Britain that a payment from the state had been given directly to women.

There was also a further shock in store for the whole country, but Manchester felt it especially as the city still had a sizeable Jewish population. The liberating armies of the Allied forces in Germany and Poland had stumbled across possibly the most shocking war crime of all time. Soldiers were unable to believe the sights which greeted them when they reached concentration camps like Auschwitz and Bergen-Belsen. There were dozens of such camps across Germany and Poland but these two had acquired a reputation for unrivalled savagery towards their inmates. People, little more than bags of bones in the infamous blue-and-white striped utility clothing used by these establishments, clung to barriers in an effort to stand upright. Equally they could not believe the sight of the liberators. Their Nazi gaolers had been brutal to the last. The 'lucky ones', if they could be called that, were at least still alive. They had survived the brutality, the beatings, the abuse, the rapes and the medical experiments, but at a terrible personal cost. Allied soldiers had tears in their eyes as they gazed at these skeletal scraps of humanity clinging to the wire fences and gave them whatever provisions they could. The full horror of what had happened emerged slowly from piecing together the prisoners' stories, interrogating captured Nazi guards, and discovering at least some of the records which the Germans had tried to destroy. Day after day trains had arrived at these camps with their human cargo loaded into cattle trucks. The trucks were unloaded, the inmates rapidly sorted into groups, and then most dispatched to the reception huts where they were ordered to undress completely and to remove any personal effects. They were then herded like cattle towards the buildings where their lives would be ended prematurely in complete and utter degradation – men, women and children. Few were spared and 6 million Jews had been killed – exterminated like vermin in huge gas chambers, as part of Hitler's 'Final Solution'. Manchester, along with the rest of the world, was stunned. Jewish folk in the city were completely traumatized. How could this be allowed to happen? Who knew? Were all Germans intrinsically evil? The answer was simply that many Germans didn't know anything about the camps until after the war was over, and when they did, most were as shocked as anyone else. Hitler, the SS and the Nazi High Command had insisted on absolute secrecy in such matters, and they had complete control of the news outlets. They did not want these activities known and anyone who did raise questions often just disappeared. Hitler had been anxious to promote a vision of the good life under the Nazis, hence his insistence on the 'model occupation' of the Channel Islands. The question now was how to deal with such terrible crimes.

In mid-March, almost two months before the European war ended, the government realized that a further call-up of military personnel would be required for the war against Japan which, at that point, showed no signs of ending. The army was now well-equipped and well-trained but the new recruits would need time to be fully trained and assimilated. Besides which it was recognized that the process of redeployment against Japan would be a complicated and difficult process. Japan's aim of bombing Pearl Harbor in 1941 was to acquire much-needed territory for its population and also raw materials such as rubber, tin and oil. The bombing of Pearl Harbor, although devastating, did not go quite to plan, leaving Japan at a disadvantage. However, they gained Hong Kong and Indo-China as well as the Malay peninsula, Singapore and the Dutch East Indies, before embarking on the infamous Burma campaign. This would give them overland access to China and enable them to cut off supplies to the army of Chiang Kai-Shek, and it would also leave them well placed to reach Assam and fan the flames of insurrection against the British Raj in India. They had entered Burma from Thailand and quickly captured Rangoon, depriving the Chinese of a supply base and port of entry. The fighting in Burma was prolonged, hot and wretched. The 1st Battalion of the Manchester Regiment, stationed in Singapore since 1938, saw action when the Japanese invaded Singapore in 1942 and, after being defeated, a number of them were taken prisoner by the Japanese who treated them badly. The 2nd Battalion of the Manchester Regiment was sent to British India in 1942 and then to Burma in 1944 where they fought in several battles before returning to India in April 1945. The Japanese were fierce fighters and Allied troops found themselves up against an enemy who was very determined, aggressive, and pretty merciless towards prisoners of war, as well as the natural enemies of snakes, scorpions, mosquitos and crocodiles. In an ironic twist of fate it was actually the Japanese who suffered the most from the crocodiles. Japanese soldiers had a strict code of honour and believed that surrender was the worst dishonour of all. Their code demanded that, if surrender became inevitable, then they should commit suicide. In February 1945, a group of Japanese soldiers fled their camp in Burma when they found themselves outflanked by invading British forces. Despite pleas from the British to surrender the Japanese attempted to cross a 10-mile-wide crocodile infested swamp to freedom. It was night and the British couldn't see much of what was happening but they heard it. About 1,000 of the Japanese soldiers were eaten by the crocodiles, an event which subsequently entered the *Guinness Book of Records* as the worst animal attack of all time. The Japanese government still refused to surrender despite the Allied call for unconditional surrender at the Potsdam Conference on 27 July. Invasion was considered but finally rejected in favour of using the as-yet untested atomic bomb. On 6 August the first atomic bomb was dropped on Hiroshima, killing 66,000 of its 255,000 citizens and injuring another 69,000, according to American figures. The Japanese still refused to surrender so the Soviet Union declared war on Japan and invaded Manchuria on 8 August, but the US had lost patience. The following day Nagasaki was bombed. Out of a population of 195,000 there were 39,000 dead and 25,000 injured, again according to American figures. Absolute figures are difficult to assess. Atomic explosions create firestorms which can cover several miles, incinerating everything in their path, and radiation sickness

VJ Day celebrations, August 1945, Rosamund Street, Chorlton-on-Medlock, Manchester. *(Courtesy of Manchester Central Library Local Studies)*

can kill many years after the event. By this time there was a division between the Japanese military who wanted to continue the fight and the civilians who simply wanted an end to the nightmare bombing and to live in peace. The Japanese emperor, Hirohito, whom many Japanese regarded as divine, had never really been in favour of the war but had had little choice except to go along with it. After the bombing of Nagasaki it was Emperor Hirohito who finally insisted that the war should end. Five days later Japan surrendered to the Allies and 14 August was designated Victory in Japan (VJ) Day. Although Manchester marked VJ Day it was not with quite the same rush of initial enthusiasm with which VE Day had been greeted, despite the Manchester Regiment's battalions having been involved in the war in the Far East.

However, an illuminated tram travelled through the city announcing the Japanese surrender; and there were celebratory gatherings in the streets with dancing on Albert Square in front of the Town Hall. Impromptu street parties were held and then everything just faded away into ordinary everyday life again. The Burma Campaign was called the 'Forgotten War' and the fighting against the Japanese in South East Asia was largely forgotten except by those who had the misfortune to endure it. The building of the bridge over the River Kwai by Allied forces was probably a better-known incident than the war itself. Nevertheless, Manchester could now tell itself that it had survived another World War and that the city had acquitted itself with honour.

Epilogue

The Second World War is not generally regarded as such a bloody affair as the Great War, although more people were killed in it. The toll in the Great War was around 38 million: 18 million deaths and 20 million wounded. The figures for the Second World War were assessed at around 60 million deaths which equalled about 3 per cent of the total world population of that time. It is more difficult to be accurate about these numbers because many bodies were totally incinerated without trace as a result of the bombing campaigns and especially the firestorms created by the atomic bombs dropped on Japan. Besides, in the Great War there were no deliberate attempts at ethnic cleansing, like the attempted extermination of the Jews in the death camps of Germany and Poland. There were fears in Britain that there would be a great deal of psychological damage caused by the bombing, the deaths and the destruction, and a number of clinics were opened to deal with the problem. But they were not needed and closed again fairly quickly. Folk did suffer from panic attacks and disturbed sleep, which were quite natural reactions to what they had experienced. A few had more serious problems but it was a tiny percentage of those affected. Many noticed, and even the Germans were moved to remark on, the British 'stoicism' during the war. The Luftwaffe, under the direction of Hermann Göring, had been initially confident that they could destroy British morale through their continuous day and night attacks in 1940–1. It didn't happen. No matter how much punishment the Germans meted out the British got back on their feet and retaliated. As someone said, '... those guys just would not lay down and die ...'. It. was as much this British attitude as the firepower and the dogfights that defeated the Luftwaffe in battles which they had expected to win. The RAF lost a large number of aircraft and crewmen but, because Britain was so highly mobilized, the British were actually manufacturing more planes than the Germans. Manchester was proud of its aircraft industry and proud too that its womenfolk played such a large part in its success during the war. Hitler himself had commented that he was unimpressed by the fact the Luftwaffe seemed to keep missing their intended targets of manufactories, roads, railways etc., blowing up civilians and churches instead. That was certainly the case in Manchester. German planes set the city alight but they did not succeed in destroying the manufacturing areas or the railway yards. It was said at the time that it was not just the result of a successful blackout, because the Luftwaffe could follow moonlight glinting on water or rails and use those to assess their targets. The Starfish sites had initially confused German bombers but that did not last long. However, on the whole, it seemed as though German military intelligence was not as good or reliable as British military intelligence, and they had no idea that the Enigma code had been cracked until long after the war was over. Towards the end of the war, although the Germans had developed early missiles with their V-1 and V-2 'flying bombs' or rockets they still were not very good at guiding them to where, from the German point of view, they would do the most damage. Only seven of the thirty-one V-1s launched at Manchester went anywhere near the city, and most of the real damage done was to a small Lancashire village and not to the manufacturing areas or marshalling yards of the city. Perhaps the inhabitants of the city had been right when they thought, in the latter part of the war, that may be there was a guardian angel keeping watch. Although Oswald Mosley survived the war, and had been released from internment in 1943, William Joyce was not so fortunate. He was executed for treason in January 1946, still defiant, still blaming the Jews for the Second World War and 'the darkness which the Jews represent' but ranting against a new enemy which he now perceived to be communism and the Soviet Union. His wife, Margaret, was spared, for the unconvincing reason that 'she had suffered enough', and she was deported to Germany where she was interned. She eventually returned to Britain, where she died, generally unmourned, in the 1970s.

After the liberation celebrations of VE Day Churchill's wartime Parliament met for the final session of its term on 15 June and a general election was called to take place on 5 July. Churchill was a stickler for the rules of the constitution and he knew that an election was long overdue. The result would not be announced for three weeks so that votes from service personnel abroad could be collected and counted. There were by now a considerable number of Labour MPs and they were determined to see the implementation of the recommendations in the Beveridge Report. Churchill was not enthusiastic, stating during his electoral campaign that:

> I must tell you that a socialist policy is abhorrent to British ideas on freedom ... A socialist state could not afford to suffer opposition – no socialist system can be established without a political police. [The Labour government] would have to fall back on some form of Gestapo'.

It was an extremely unfortunate choice of words, linking a Labour government to the Gestapo, especially in a city like Manchester where thousands of its young men had witnessed, first Franco's henchmen, and then Hitler's henchmen. Churchill himself had been instrumental in getting Mosley's Blackshirts disbanded and now it seemed that he was tarring socialists, who had done nothing to deserve it, with the same brush. There had been a coalition government throughout the war and Churchill had received the necessary support from Labour MPs. Members of the Labour Party had more than pulled their weight on the Home Front. Soldiers, sailors and airmen who held Labour beliefs had fought hard for their country. Labour Party members and believers in socialist principles had given their all to defeat fascism every bit as much as Conservatives. Britain had been hailed as the most mobilized country in the war. Its female population had thrown themselves into the war effort, ably supporting and assisting the male population. This was supposedly the secret of its success and eventual victory. Furthermore, there had been no mention by the Conservatives of implementing anything contained in the Beveridge Report. Clement Attlee, the leader of the Labour Party, seized the moment, and he had been quite unequivocal in his proposals for the future. Labour's manifesto (entitled 'Let Us Face the Future') contained proposals to nationalize the Bank of England, fuel and power, inland transport and iron and steel. Government intervention would be necessary, the party argued, to keep a check on raw materials, food prices and employment. Following the Beveridge Report of 1942, the Labour Party also formed plans to create a National Health Service and social security.

Unsurprisingly Labour won a landslide victory with an overall majority of 146. Churchill was shocked and felt betrayed. He could not believe that he had led the British people successfully through the biggest war in history only to have them turn their backs on him.

The facts were a little more prosaic. Churchill was an excellent wartime leader. That was his time. He was not a peacetime leader. His bulldog attitude, his impatience and his often harsh dismissal of issues and ideas were not suited to the changing society which was evolving after the war. This was Clement Attlee's time.

Shortly after the capitulation of the Japanese and the celebration of VJ Day (15 August 1945) the United Nations was established and its charter ratified on 24 October. Britain was one of the five Security Council members and had a power of veto.

An event of national and international importance was held in Manchester on 15–21 October 1945. In 1944 the Pan-African Federation had been formed by an association of black people living and working in Manchester to tackle the problems that European colonialism had created and the resulting racial discrimination against black people whose countries and labour the Europeans had plundered extensively.

Its main aims were to:

- To promote the well-being and unity of African peoples and peoples of African descent throughout the world.
- To demand self-determination and independence of African peoples ... from the domination of powers claiming sovereignty and trusteeship over them.
- To secure equality of civil rights for African peoples and the abolition of all forms of racism.

There had been a number of Pan-African conferences held but this one, the fifth, was held in Manchester because its citizens were recognized as politically active and aware of such issues. They had, after all, supported Abraham Lincoln in his fight against slavery, although at great cost to themselves. Africans had fought on the side of the Allies during the war and felt that they had earned their independence from the mostly hated colonial rule. The conference was organized by George Padmore from Trinidad and Kwame Nkrumah, the independence leader from Ghana. There were ninety delegates of whom twenty-six were from Africa, including independence leader Jomo Kenyatta of Kenya, Hastings Banda from Malawi, and representatives from Nigeria and Jamaica. The West Indies sent thirty-three delegates and there were thirty-five delegates from British organizations. Although hardly mentioned in the British press a number of important resolutions were passed regarding racial discrimination, imperialism and capitalism.

The National Insurance Act (1946) was passed, as promised, in that year, creating unemployment, sickness, maternity and pension benefits paid for by employees, employers and the state, and on 1 January 1947 the British coal industry was nationalized. There were still severe fuel shortages which meant that BDST was re-established for the summer of 1947.

The war had also forced Britain to realize that it was no longer viable to maintain a global empire and on 15 August 1947 India was granted its independence from Britain. Unable to find a solution acceptable to both Muslims and Hindus the country was partitioned into India and Pakistan which caused a number of problems that, seventy years later, have yet to be fully resolved. Perhaps the most major post-war innovation came on 5 July 1948 when the National Health Service (NHS) was established, spearheaded by the Minister of Health, Aneurin (Nye) Bevan. For the first time in history medical treatment was freely available to everyone. The changes inaugurated by Clement Attlee's Labour government in the immediate post-war years changed the face of daily life in Britain. Much of the 'old order' disappeared. The country-house lifestyle of lavish parties and daily extravagances, while servants below stairs were paid a pittance, were over, and so too were the days of slavery in the 'satanic mills'. Workers were given reasonable hours and reasonable wages. Slums began to be cleared and new housing built. Initially this was in the form of pre-fabricated housing which was cheap and easy to build. The slogan 'she can't make a home until she gets one' was used to encourage the promotion of affordable housing. A much wider range of occupations was now open to women. Education and opportunity were available to everyone. There suddenly seemed to be lots of exciting possibilities. To paraphrase Aldous Huxley, there really was a brave new world to face.

Index